Adam

Only if you agree with
just one topic will
my life have any purpose
and meaning.

Looking forward to your
critical review.

Hurrah for the Red
and the Blue.

Love to All

TABLE OF CONTENTS

A MORE PERFECT UNION

UNIFYING IDEAS FOR A
Divided America

DAVID GOTTSTEIN

TRUSTED PUBLISHING LLC

Trusted Publishing, LLC
P.O. Box 90530 Anchorage, Alaska, 99509-0530

ISBN: 978-0-578-24010-7

Library of Congress Control Number: 2020922943

Cover Photo © 2021 www.gettyimages.com. All rights reserved - used with permission.

PRINTED IN THE UNITED STATES OF AMERICA

INTRODUCTION

I am excited about America. But I am also concerned that we are falling behind our potential in many ways. I am not a politician or an aspiring elected official. I am, however, a hard-working small business owner with the privilege of having had an Ivy League education, who has also been a political activist at the state and national level for decades. And I am one who believes that our government is best protected by an informed citizenry that participates in our democratic processes. I have decided that perhaps the most effective way I could hope to have an impact would be to write this book. What I am hoping to accomplish is to start a serious conversation regarding one or more of the ideas I will advance.

I am sixty-five years old, a proud father, a successful businessman, a trained economist and Registered Investment Advisor who, as a fiduciary, manages retirement accounts for mostly middle-class Americans. I am also an inventor of financial services software, a political activist, and an American patriot with a private pilot's license. This is a book that speaks to the greatness of America, and how we can aspire to and attain even greater heights in human achievement, including equality for all. Be that thousand points of light. This book is my soapbox on which to stand,

and is a collection of public policy ideas on what a more perfect Union might look like, and how we can get there.

A more perfect Union would be one where every child is loved, nurtured, and provided equal access to a quality education, healthcare, housing, and justice. A place where they can secure a job that allows them to reach their full potential, receiving a fair day's wage for a fair day's work. And if you're fully able-bodied, and need resources in order to survive because you don't have inherited wealth, then you should work and provide for yourself. To the extent people have work disabilities, they should be provided for. And those who are fully able to work, and choose not to, should go hungry, until they do so, so that we don't invite lethargy and dependency on the efforts of hard-working taxpayers. Anything short of that means that because people aren't allowed to reach their own potential, we as a nation don't reach our full potential, and there is less for everybody to go around, and we are all worse off. I believe these are the virtues that I share with most Americans. To a great extent, it is our purpose. And it certainly represents a much more perfect Union than exists today. I believe that if we were to pick the three most important roles of government, the first would be to protect our safety from both foreign and domestic forces. The second would be to provide the environment for a vibrant, fair and just capitalistic marketplace, in order to motivate and reward hard work and risk taking. And third, to reduce suffering by helping to lift the most people out of poverty.

I believe the Black Lives Matters movement is more than a massive effort to heighten national awareness of the systemic disadvantages and mistreatment too often suffered largely by people of color, particularly African Americans. It is also a symptom of the suffering and despair that is an outcome of the vast and growing disparity of wealth and lack of opportunity not only in our country, but around the world. I believe the global response to George Floyd's murder was not only a sympathy march, but also a response to peoples own suffering at the hands of the power elite.

Here in America, President Donald Trump fed the narrative that the misfortunes suffered by white Have-Nots is the fault of the Have-Nots of color. After generations of being targeted by systemic racism, people of color, supported by a majority of white Americans have had enough. And while this struggle between the white Have-Nots, and the Have-Nots of color has progressed, the Have's keep making more money, and creating more advantage for themselves.

It is first critically important that we start from the common understanding and appreciation that everything good about the good old U.S.A. comes through the blood and sacrifices of the U.S. soldier. Liberty, freedom, property rights, the rule of law, equal justice under the law, freedom of assembly, and the freedom to enjoy the fruits of our own labor without fear of confiscation, all comes through the sacrifices, past, present, and future, of the brave and courageous young men and women of the armed forces. We, and those who have lived before us, are blessed and honored to be protected by this historic all volunteer army. I try and thank as many of them as I can. And I encourage you to do so as well. We owe them almost EVERYTHING.

As a culture, we strive to achieve greatness on a continuous basis. And generally speaking, it has worked pretty darn well. We defeated the Nazis and the Japanese at the same time. We went to the moon, and have landed lots of hardware on Mars. There is nothing we can't achieve that is humanly possible, because America defines what is humanly possible.

Still, far too many millions of Americans are being left behind. And there are reasons for that we must resolve to understand and overcome in order to be those thousand points of light, and that beacon on the hill. The rise in populism is a direct response to excessive success that the wealthy have achieved economically and politically, at the expense of pretty much everybody else. Hopefully we can get to a more just and pluralistic balance. That is what this book is largely about, from a domestic policy point of view. The reason for the reversal in social justice, I believe, has been magnified by the decay in our political system and decision-making process. And the money influences that helped make it so. In order to reverse those forces, we need to first understand them.

The purpose of this book, in large part, is an attempt to try and pierce through the paid and influenced media, as well as our social media bubbles to bring to the national discussion, some out-of-the-box "more perfect Union" ideas. Ideas that can hopefully make what is still the greatest country in the history of the planet, an even better one; grounded in liberty, egalitarianism, humanism, the rule of law, and a meritocracy.

This book is largely an attempt to identify the major problems facing our country, and to offer new directions for Americans to think about and discuss in a national political debate. So that in some small way our collective thinking may change enough so that we can nudge our way back to being closer to the vision of a meritocracy that our Founding Fathers crafted for us. Hopefully we can fully unleash the power of individual hard work, risk taking, achievement and unbounded just rewards. If I didn't think we could, I wouldn't have written this book.

I come from a politically active family, and have myself been a political activist for over fifty years. That's because I recognize the importance of having qualified people from the private sector participating in our election and legislative processes. There are millions of Americans like myself who choose to try and make a difference by participating in elections and advocating for change. An engaged and informed citizenry is critical to the success of a democracy.

Can we fix ourselves? I believe we can. We can, and we must. If America is going to survive as a place of opportunity for all, it is going to require real leadership. It won't be easy. But the truthful, just, and American way of life that our forefathers envisioned for us, that the greatest generation fought and died for, and was the envy of the world, has the capacity to reinvent its greatness.

This is why I decided to write this book. I am an ordinary patriotic American, who loves his country, but who is disappointed in it. And I am hoping that at least one idea in this book will reach the national consciousness, and be acted upon. If so, it will have been worth it.

CHAPTER 1

OUR DEMOCRACY, THE BEST THAT MONEY CAN BUY

Winston Churchill famously quipped, "Democracy is the worst form of government, except for all others." Absolute power corrupts absolutely, and therefore it is only a citizen government that can protect citizens against its own government. Enduring benevolent dictatorships and dynasties simply don't exist.

Churchill is also credited with saying "America will always do the right thing, after it exhausts all other options." Though there is no record of the British Prime Minister ever making or writing the statement, it has been repeated so often as to find a permanent home in the American political lexicon. Unfortunately, the continuous stream of other options that we are enduring during this period of time in our history is exhausting, because we are failing and under-performing in still too many critically important ways.

In fact, the center of our problems is political in nature. It is not with Americans ourselves. Money has always been a key part of the political landscape in America. And it always will be. We can't escape that. But it is how we have evolved in letting deep-pocketed individuals and corporations dominate political spending that is a core problem. It is why we have huge technology corporations, even now worth trillions of dollars, that dominate their market segments, for example, limiting choice and protections for the consumer.

I am sixty-five years old and recently enrolled in Medicare. I am old enough to remember watching the Nixon-Kennedy debate. I didn't understand the issues at the time, or the importance of the event. But I remember my parents watching it on a flickering black and white TV.

I believe the beginning of our political problems began with that 1960 debate. Richard Nixon was the sitting Vice-President, and was thought to have the advantage. John Kennedy was a young U.S. Senator and a war hero, but also a Catholic, so he was considered the underdog.

But under the hot studio lights, Nixon perspired. A lot. It made him appear perhaps more nervous than he was, and the camera amplified every flaw. In contrast, JFK was poised, had make-up applied, and came across as a confident and strong leader. That debate changed the tide of the campaign, the outcome of the election, and the course of human history. We went to the moon. But it also, in my view, represented the inflection point in a change in the political landscape of America.

As I mentioned, it is the point in time where paid media, and its growing cost, began to largely influence the outcomes of elections. The result is that eventually our political campaigns have succumbed to the special interests, corporate and otherwise, with deep enough pockets and the financial capacity to pay for very expensive media and ground campaigns. It is transforming an America now shaped by special interests rather than the middle-class and common man…and woman.

The Supreme Court decision known as Citizens United in 2010, which gave free speech rights to corporations equal to that of individuals, has accelerated the influence of the rich and powerful in our election processes. The money comes from both sides, from the Koch brothers on the right, to George Soros on the left, and hundreds of corporations and Super-PACS in between. One of the popular liberal jokes at the time was that we would know that corporations are the same as people when Texas executes one. But it is no joke now.

In the spirit of full disclosure, I am not a member of any organized party. I'm a Democrat. Or at least, I used to think of myself as one. But my party has left me in many respects. I am in my 55th year of political activism, having started stuffing envelopes for the "All the Way with LBJ" campaign in 1964. I was ten years old. I got involved because my father, Barney Gottstein, and his business partner Larry Carr, who built a successful grocery operation in Alaska during the 1970s and 1980s, were the largest Democratic fundraisers in the State of Alaska. It wasn't until I was in my twenties that I learned you could invite people to your home and not charge them money.

Jimmy Carter, at the onset of his presidential run, crashed a birthday party at our family home for our then U.S. Senator Mike Gravel during the summer of 1975. When he reached the top of the stairs, Carter reached out and shook my hand, and said, "Hi, my name is Jimmy Carter, and I'm running for president." I have been honored to have met other presidents, or would-be presidents, including Gerald Ford, Barack Obama, and Joe Biden.

But my party isn't speaking to me these days, on many issues, as it strays from its historical understanding of capitalism, and America's role in the world. And the Republicans aren't doing so well either. Like millions of Americans, I am thinking independently of the party platforms that are offered to us. I am most interested in those candidates who are advocating and working toward the right policies, and who can work across the aisle and reach compromises that can work for most everybody.

I have an equally offensive description of both parties: Republicans spend all of their time trying to make sure the economic pie is as big as it can possibly be without making sure everybody has an opportunity for a slice, while Democrats assume the pie exists and start cutting it up, and giving it away. Each approach, I believe, is just about equally wrong.

I have been involved in dozens of campaigns at all levels of government. I have supported Democrats and Republicans, depending upon who I thought was the best candidate at the time. I strongly believe the more that individual Americans get involved, the better our government can still be. But it needs to include those who are operating for the greater good—those looking to protect America's future and not just secure their own political fortunes. Those who will put their constituents' interests ahead of special interests.

One of the biggest problems of course is the very high cost of campaigns. A United States senator with a campaign budget of $10,000,000, not an unheard-of amount nowadays, has to have his or her hand out with the need to raise over $30,000 for each of the 312 weeks they are in office for each six-year term. Then multiply that budget for senators from New York, California and Florida. There are a lot of handouts going both ways. It is just human nature for a person to listen more to someone who is giving them money than to those who are not. Money buys access. We can't change that. That by itself doesn't make an elected official bad or corrupt. But it shouldn't buy votes, or contracts, or special language in a bill. However, all too often, it does.

When I was a young man in my twenties, I was privileged to work as an aide to an Alaska state senate president by the name of Jalmar Kerttula, who went by Jay. He became a mentor of mine. Jay was as honest and pro good government as they get. A farmer by trade, his family came to Alaska at the invitation of FDR, during the Great Depression. He taught me how politics worked behind the scenes, as I was a fixture in his office for almost five months. Jay taught me that you have to give up things you want in order to get things you need. And that by working across the aisle, a lot can be accomplished. With that, and by always being an honest broker, one can achieve a significant amount of political capital within the legislature and gain a lot for one's constituency.

So that is where we start the discussion. It isn't a pretty picture of late. We are a long way from the days when Democrats and Republicans would attack each other on the House or Senate floor, and then go share a pitcher of beer or a glass of scotch at the end of the day. But we are where we are.

I will continue to support candidates who pledge to work across the aisle and place principle over party. And I encourage you to do the same in an effort to restore our democracy—the worst form of government, except for all others.

CHAPTER 2

THE CLIMES, THEY ARE A CHANGING

How New Energy Can Save Our Planet

Accepting the science on climate change and taking the necessary steps to reverse its impact is probably the most important thing we can do in the interest of a more perfect Union. I understand that this is a grandiose statement, but most people, in my experience, when they take the time to become informed, agree. It is a challenge that can be hard to visualize, but is as important as was America going to the moon. Maybe even more important.

Now, I am not a scientist, and I never played one on TV, but there is something most of us can agree on. Our planet is changing. It is getting warmer. The climate is changing. It is undeniable, and undebatable. I can't tell you how much of it might be part of a natural weather cycle, or how much human activity is accelerating it. I don't think anybody knows for sure. Is climate change caused by humans by a measure of 10%, or is it closer to 90%? Maybe it's somewhere in between. Regardless of the level of impact we are having on the climate, the climate is definitely having a major impact on us. Therefore, we humans should take serious responsibility for at least a material portion of climate change and do the things necessary to try and reverse it or at the very least slow it down considerably.

Why must we take climate change seriously and take commensurate action? Because we're killing the planet, or at least making it un-inhabitable for humans, and many other species, in certain places of the world. The Chinese can't breathe their air. As the ice caps melt, the oceans are rising and risk flooding vast amounts of coastal populations. The oceans are warming. Weather patterns are changing, resulting in storms with increased frequency and intensity. As the waters warm, they starve the oceans of oxygen, leaving dead zones that no longer support marine life. Life cycles and migratory patterns of ocean species are changing, threatening their very survival.

My home state of Alaska is on the leading edge of climate change. Our winters and summers are clearly trending warmer. Permafrost, the frozen soil that covers 85% of Alaska, is melting after millions of years of having been frozen. Villages are falling into the oceans and rivers due to increased erosion, and in some cases are having to be moved. The migratory patterns of sea and land mammals are changing.

During the summer of 2019, Anchorage hit 90 degrees for the first time in recorded history. And alarmingly, Alaska was on fire that summer with more than 600 wildfires burning the month of August alone. In fact, some fires were not extinguished by the winter snowpack. They continued to burn below ground throughout the winter only to surface again the following summer. That is how hot the planet has become.

It is no longer reasonable to deny that our climate is changing, and that the world is getting warmer. There is also no doubt that the growth in the burning of fossil fuels has impacted the ozone layer and the amount of heat being held in our atmosphere. Without action the world will become warmer, dirtier, and less inhabitable.

Hopefully by now I have convinced you there might be a very big problem. But what is the solution? Certainly, we should all recycle, drive fuel-efficient cars or electric cars, take public transportation, and generally waste less. But the real culprit is energy. Particularly oil and coal. But even natural gas helps to increase our human-produced carbon footprint and contributes to climate change and global warming. The bunker fuel used in most ocean-going freighters causes an ungodly amount of highly polluting and dirty exhaust.

The solution is that the world needs to wean itself from burning hydrocarbons as a principal energy source. Instead we need to use the energy that is all around us in the form of wind, solar, geo-thermal, tidal, and hydro principally. There is even technology in use today that can generate energy just from the change in ocean water temperatures at various ocean depths. There is enough energy all around us to replace fossil fuels. We just haven't figured out how to make it usable on a grand scale. Yet.

This, I believe is our new moonshot goal: a world that allows people to turn the lights on, and run our factories when the sun goes down, and the wind stops, by efficiently producing and storing the natural energy that is all around us. Success will be measured in terms of energy storage cost efficiencies, energy decay over time, as well as production that is as benign to the planet as possible. We need to evolve and advance such that these renewable resources can be used as our primary source for base power and not just for supplemental energy.

The first step in achieving this new level of energy independence is solving the energy storage problem.

If we can store energy that can be generated from all the sources I mentioned, very, very, cheaply, then we have the opportunity to save the

planet. We have come a long way in terms of transporting electricity efficiently with our advances in super-conductivity. But our batteries would
need to be at least a hundred times more efficient than they are today in
order to solve the mass energy storage problem.

We should all appreciate the efforts of Elon Musk, the genius head
of the Tesla Motor company, who is building electric cars with advanced
battery technology being developed in-house. But it isn't good enough.
I am sorry, Elon. Not by a moonshot, if we are going to save the planet
in time. Why? Because the energy being stored in Elon's batteries is produced principally from, you guessed it, natural gas and coal. Fossil fuels.
Even electric cars have a carbon footprint and climatic impact today.

The good news is that even with today's somewhat high economic
barriers for energy storage devices, industrial-sized battery facilities tied
to wind and solar farms are being built in order that they may be used as
base power. But it isn't enough, and it isn't happening fast enough to save
us, and our planet.

We need a battery or energy storage technology that can store massive
amounts of energy to be called upon anytime. Very cheaply. We need a
global effort on the scale of the Manhattan Project, which developed the
atomic bomb in record time.

How might we accomplish this miracle? First, let's understand what
really has to happen, from a scientific point of view. We need to accomplish at least two quantum leaps of scientific advancement. That is because
our science hasn't yet advanced far enough for us to even know what new
directions and multiple scientific breakthroughs that will be necessary in
order to be successful. And we need to greatly accelarate the timeline. In
other words, only through inventiveness, trial and error, acceptance of repeated failures, accidental discoveries, and high risk-taking will we achieve
a stream of technological breakthroughs that will give us the means and

ability to take the science to the next level. It might take three or even four quantum leaps to get there. We must take those risks, just like we did in developing the atomic bomb and going to the moon. We need to spend those collective resources, and do so smartly, if we are going to leave succeeding generations with a fully inhabitable planet.

Some say that nuclear fusion reactors are the way to go. Fusion reactors theoretically produce energy similar to traditional fission reactors, but without the problem of generating long-lived radioactive waste. This might be a reasonable ancillary path, but it shouldn't be assumed or expected to be our primary solution. It still might be too dangerous, and costly. We should pursue it, but not rely on it as our energy savior.

How do we accomplish the necessary technological leaps? It comes from good old basic research. Much of the research and development in the private sector is designed to accomplish known or desired outcomes. The amount spent is commensurate with the projected return. Therefore, the amount expected to be earned will pay for the research, with a tidy profit.

But unbounded basic research is different, meaning that it need not adhere to normal profit requirements, but instead to technology goals, which is imperative in this case. It is how we made it to the moon. No corporation could have afforded to take the risk on its own to figure out how to build the Saturn V rocket that took us to the moon. Instead, our whole country took the collective risk necessary to reach for the stars, stopping on the moon along the way. This all happened because of a national commitment to succeed. It was accomplished through a collaboration made possible through high federal government spending along with corporate and academic partners that profited and contributed along the way.

The non-government entities didn't have the capacity to take the risk, but the federal government did. Basic research, to be really basic, needs the luxury of being wrong, over and over again, and to be able to persevere. Scientists need to be able to try what might appear to be crazy ideas, and fail. They must be encouraged to take risks and not get fired for failure, and to be paid for trying so that in the end, new discoveries are made through the result of systematic trial and error and sometimes by accident.

When John F. Kennedy challenged our nation to go to the moon in less than ten years, we wrote a blank check. And we did it. Maybe we generated the will necessary to achieve the moonshot science as a legacy to our assassinated and beloved leader. We can't afford a blank check anymore. And there appears to be little will to do this as a country, on our own. So be it. But it is an urgent global threat that promises colossal consequences in the decades and centuries ahead if we don't take big action soon.

Corporate America can't do it on its own. The rewards aren't visible enough, or soon enough for the executives to reap the benefits through the exercising of stock options by the time they retire. Even our major corporations don't have either the capital or the incentive to do it on their own because the risks outweigh the rewards, in pure economic terms, over customary investment time horizons. But the rewards to the world's population are not just economic. How much is saving the planet worth? Almost anything, I would argue.

How then do we achieve the multiple quantum scientific leaps that will be necessary in order to accomplish this critical undertaking? How do we change the risk and reward equation to make it happen? How do we generate the massive amount of capital necessary for the scientific research? How can we assemble the right combination of resources in order to achieve this Holy Grail of technological advancement?

We do so by unleashing the greatness of America to solve it by harnessing our inventiveness, hard work, risk-taking, ingenuity, teamwork, and the capital formation capabilities of our great nation. In other words, we put into play the greatest and most productive market mechanism ever invented by humans: the American capitalistic system.

It might sound too simple, but I believe very strongly that it can work. But our leaders must have the courage to lead. America must lead the funding effort component necessary to change the basic research risk versus reward calculus in a significant enough way, sufficient to provide the economic catalyst to jump-start the process. And we should be joined by Great Britain, France, Germany, South Korea, China, Canada, Australia, Japan, and others, to fund the mother of all contests.

These countries, and more if possible, should underwrite a scientific contest. The first collection of corporate, academic, and scientific enterprises able to solve the energy storage problem to a set of required specifications will receive a check for one trillion dollars. That's trillion. With a "T." And the winner will own a portion of the economic rights to the technology. Even if the prize is twice that amount, it will be worth it. What will be the cost of replacing all of the cities around the world that will be under water in a hundred years?

When and if this contest starts, watch what happens in a rational market economy. It will start an immediate race. On your mark, get set... go! As a result, I predict the private sector will figure it out in ten to fifteen years. That is because the winning team will get paid big, paid twice, and therefore the whole risk versus reward ratio gets dramatically improved. It will be paid first by the government for accomplishing the task, and second from the market through royalties when the global solution gets delivered to the marketplace. It would dwarf even the success of the iPhone.

I wouldn't be surprised if competing global consortiums even combine at some point, as the market recognizes the synergies and values of scientific collaboration. It might take more than ten to fifteen years. It might be a different prize value that sets the race in motion. We have spent more than a trillion dollars in the Middle East over the last thirty years fighting wars. In just the past year the U.S. alone has spent trillions on pandemic related efforts. Elon Musk just successfully delivered American astronauts to and from the International Space Station, as a for-profit enterprise, with government support. American ingenuity is amazing when properly incentivized.

What could an energy storage world look like? No carbon emissions. Clean skies. Breathable air. Stable oceans. Whole new industries. We could even place millions of acres of solar panels on the ocean surfaces sufficient to absorb enough of the sun's heat to not only provide power for millions of people, but manage the temperature of the oceans so that we stop baking them.

This idea therefore is the perhaps the biggest and most important idea to be offered in the book, because it affects the lives of all current and future global inhabitants. There is no future to cooking our planet by burning hydrocarbons. I will dedicate myself to this endeavor, and I invite you to participate in this critically important geo-political task. Climate change is global, and so too must be its solution. It's only a matter of life and death.

CHAPTER 3

WATER, WATER EVERYWHERE

Almost fifty years ago, Dustin Hoffman's character in the movie *The Graduate* was told that plastics were the next big thing. It was good advice because of the emerging market for a vibrant set of products made from oil and gas hydrocarbons. Today, I think, the next big thing is water. Fresh water, potable water, desalinated water, and unpolluted water.

There are three key elements to achieving water security for the future. The first is tied to the previous idea. If we solve the energy storage problem, allowing us to collect, transport, and store benign natural energy, then we will also be able to desalinate the oceans inexpensively and provide ample drinkable water for most of the world's population, with enough left over to meet the needs of agriculture.

Secondly, everybody deserves enough clean drinking water in order to sustain their lives, at as low a price as possible. Any water consumed beyond meeting our drinking needs should be priced closer to the marginal cost of delivering it, but at a price high enough so that we incorporate a logical rationing market mechanism into the water marketplace equation. The economics of zero or subsidized pricing encourages waste. Charging a replacement or marginal cost of water above our primary human consumption needs will also help determine the most valuable and important uses for the freshest water. There is a huge battle going on in the West where residents compete with agricultural and other commercial interests for water rights, and states compete with other states.

The Colorado River is at the center of this battle for water security. Seven western states, along with Mexico, have signed agreements to share the Colorado's water. At the time the Colorado River Compact was signed nearly one hundred years ago, there were fewer homes, fewer farms, and plenty of surplus water. But that is no longer the case.

California still gets the largest percentage of the Colorado's water, but it is not nearly enough to quench the thirst of its 40 million residents. That's why California is embracing the promise of desalination.

Today, more than 300 million people around the world get their water from desalination plants, according to the International Desalination Association. The largest desalination plant in America sits in Carlsbad, California just north of San Diego, turning 100 million gallons of the Pacific Ocean into 50 million gallons of fresh water every day. It provides roughly 10 percent of the fresh water needs of 3 million Californians. And it is just one of eleven desalination plants in California currently operating, with another eleven on the drawing board.

Although desalination shows great promise, the cost/benefit ratio is still a little muddy. First of all, it's expensive—roughly twice the cost of water from the Colorado River. And, because it takes a lot of energy to desalinate sea water, the carbon footprint is significant. The carbon footprint of the Carlsbad plant, for example, is estimated to be about 61,000 metric tons annually. In other parts of the world, where power is generated almost exclusively from oil and natural gas, the impact is even greater.

Then there's the question of what to do with the 50 million gallons of briny water left over after the process. Remember, it takes two gallons of seawater to create one gallon of fresh water. If the leftover briny water is not disposed of properly by diffusing it over a wide area in the Pacific, it can deplete oxygen levels, threatening an already stressed ocean ecosystem.

The good news is that technology continues to make the promise of desalination cheaper and more ecologically friendly. The cost of desalination has dropped by more than half over the past thirty years. And as we generate more of our power from renewable sources, desalination's carbon footprint will shrink as well. The tide might just be turning.

I believe we have another option, one that mirrors one of America's greatest achievements of the last 100 years. Consider, as our climate has changed, much of the U.S. has experienced significant changes in precipitation patterns over the last twenty-five years. Our warming planet is shifting rainfall patterns, most noticeably in the Northeast, Midwest, and parts of the Southeast. These areas are receiving much more precipitation than they need in order to maintain water supplies, with periods of flooding, especially along the Mississippi River. During the researching and writing of this book, Texas, Louisiana, Florida, and elsewhere have suffered greatly from flooding. For the third time in ten years, the city of Houston was underwater.

Meanwhile, since 2000, the West has experienced one of its driest twenty-year periods in history. A recent Columbia University study suggests the nine-state region from Montana to New Mexico may be entering a period of mega-drought not seen in 12-hundred years.

Is it possible to solve both problems at once? Can we provide relief to a waterlogged East and a parched West simultaneously? I believe we can.

Imagine a secure interstate water system capable of transporting large amounts of water from those areas most vulnerable to flooding, to where the water is needed. It simply requires the same vision that President

Eisenhower had when he paved the way for the country's interstate high-way system. A secure system, positioned strategically to bring the extra water and rainfall that large parts of the country have to areas like the Southwest, where populations and industries are too often under severe stress from prolonged droughts.

This would be a massive public works project that would employ perhaps hundreds of thousands of people for at least ten to twenty years. It might do for America what the aqueducts did for Rome. The combination of desalination and an interstate water system just might provide water security for hundreds of years. As you'll see in our next chapter, it could also solve another pressing failure that has prevented us from being a more perfect Union.

CHAPTER 4

IN DEFENSE OF A LIVING WAGE

Right behind the need to protect our country from outside forces, and along with creating opportunity for all, I believe it is a moral imperative to help people out of poverty. I believe it is a quintessential American value. And I would suggest in that noble quest, the most meaningful path would be to have the U.S. Government be the employer of last resort for work ready U.S. citizens, at a living wage. The living wage should be high enough that two parents, for example, working full time, could support a family of four above the poverty line—a wage that provides the basics of food, clothing, and shelter, along with access to transportation and basic health care without further government assistance.

We can afford to help those in need, who cannot do for themselves. That too is well within our ability and value set as Americans. But it is not an American value to support those who choose not to work. To the extent the fully able-bodied, or partially able-bodied, are able enough to provide a service, they should be required to do so. If an able-bodied person chooses not to work at a government-provided job, then there should be no government assistance.

For much of the past nine years, any American looking for a job had a good chance of finding one. The unemployment rate was a meager 3.5% as recently as February of 2020. By April, the jobless rate approached 15%. The COVID-19 pandemic put millions out of work, resulting in more than 30 million Americans receiving jobless benefits. It's impossible to know, as of this writing, how the pandemic will change America's unemployment picture, but recovery will likely be slow. Many small businesses will be out of business. Many large corporations will not survive. For those that do, their workforce will likely be smaller. Many companies will have discovered the cost benefits of having employees work from home. We must be prepared for a large part of America's workforce without jobs.

I want to be clear in stating that this guaranteed employment program would apply only to bona fide U.S. citizens who are qualified and work ready. It isn't intended to be a social welfare program, or mental health program, both of which should be administered under different mandates. We also don't want it to be a magnet for the world's poor. It would be a program that provides government jobs where they are needed. If a person is able-bodied, they should be working for pay, instead of receiving welfare. Workfare, not welfare.

There is a precedence for this kind of guaranteed employment program. The Works Progress Administration put millions of Americans to work in the 1930s building thousands of roads, bridges, buildings, and dams. The WPA allowed Americans to lift themselves out of poverty and provided the transportation and interstate power infrastructure still in use today. The Bureau of Reclamation built the Hoover Dam. Imagine a modern WPA tasked with building that massive interstate water system. The WPA ended with the advent of America's entry into World War II. Unemployment was no longer an issue as the country threw itself into military service and building the instruments of war.

The COVID-19 pandemic is a war-like event that has cost lives and jobs, without the opportunity to employ large numbers of Americans to fight the outbreak. It created few winners and many losers. The result will be large numbers of traditional blue-collar and white-collar workers without jobs to return to.

We will have to be creative and look for the opportunities to put Americans back to work. Beyond the manual labor required to repair America's infrastructure, we could provide affordable child-care programs for working mothers and fathers and programs to assist the elderly or the blind. Many of these programs could be managed as a public sector/private sector partnership providing a minimum wage that is a living wage, and providing a societal value for a federal dollar that a welfare dollar does not.

I will argue that a minimum wage that is less than what a working couple can live on represents a form of labor exploitation. And it can plant seeds of resentment, and lead to a form of class warfare. A fair society will want its hard-working and unskilled and semi-skilled workers to be part of the success story of the wider community. Workers just starting out in the workforce who are able to produce at an energetic level for forty hours a week deserve to be fed, clothed, and sheltered, along with having access to other basic human needs. That's not a handout. A minimum wage that offers the opportunity for survival, accomplishment, and dignity should be a human right in the land of opportunity. Therefore, a fair minimum wage makes sense, one that provides for basic human needs.

The very concept of a minimum wage has proven controversial. Perhaps a good place to start is to ask why some people might be opposed to the idea of even raising the minimum wage to a living wage. The main argument often used against raising the minimum wage is that it is a job destroyer because it will make it too difficult for many businesses to make a profit if their manpower costs rise without matching price increases. In a price-sensitive world, it is argued, they would lose business. The result, detractors say, is that many employees would have to be fired, and fewer people hired.

Another seemingly valid argument is that by raising the wages for the lowest and most unskilled workers, those with greater skills will have to get a raise, if they were being paid at or below the new minimum wage.

Let me start the rebuttal by saying that even Henry Ford knew he had to pay his own workers enough to be able to buy the cars they were building. That ushered in a big jump in wages to $5 per day at a minimum, for Ford workers. A rising tide lifts all boats. Trickle-up works. Trickle-down leaves far too many behind.

A wage policy designed to get people out of poverty will result in much less public assistance. That can usher in a cultural shift away from an entitlement mentality. What each of us should be entitled to is the opportunity to work hard and to provide for our families. If you are an able-bodied person and capable of contributing to the country's economic engine, you are more obligated to feed yourself than to have other people feed you.

How much in public assistance do Walmart workers receive because they don't get paid enough to live on? Tens of thousands have to rely on food stamps just to survive. That can be largely eliminated with an increase in the minimum wage and a guaranteed job. Instead of the public paying a material amount of Walmart's labor costs through welfare transfer payments, the consumers of the products they sell will appropriately be paying it instead.

A business paying a $15 an hour minimum wage would be competing on a level playing field when their competitors have the same employee cost burden. In the case of restaurants, where tips often represent a large portion of a worker's compensation, then a portion of tips can be included in the minimum wage calculation.

A livable minimum wage impact is kind of like the impact of the price of oil going up in large energy consumption business like airlines. It doesn't put one airline at a disadvantage to another. As long as a market participant has to pay the same amount as their competitor for basic expenses like labor, then they will have to rely on other economic efficiencies and service in order to attract business and make more money. That is a good thing. Any restaurant jobs that are lost because families decide to eat at home more cheaply than eating out will result in more jobs at the local grocery stores. There could be a reduced minimum wage rate for teenage workers, since teenagers tend to be less skilled and less productive. But there should still be a place for them in the workforce.

Just how big of an impact would a minimum wage have on the overall economy? According to the U.S. Bureau of Labor Statistics, in 2014, 77.2 million workers age 16 and older in the United States were paid hourly rates, representing 58.7 % of all wage and salary workers. Among those paid by the hour, 1.3 million earned exactly the prevailing federal minimum wage of $7.25 per hour. That is less than 2% of the hourly workforce. Even a liberal calculation of the number of workers who would be directly impacted by having their wages raised to a new minimum wage would be less than 5%. If you add the workers currently making minimum wage who would expect to receive a similar increase, you might be raising wages for 10% of the workforce, but certainly not more.

That's a modest price to pay to get hard-working Americans out of poverty through hard work. We should properly reform our welfare programs to workfare. I believe paying workers less than it costs to sustain life is a form of human exploitation. In the end, if government assistance is required because a livable hourly rate isn't being paid, then taxpayers are subsidizing an insufficient minimum wage, without the benefit of the product or service. As consumers, we should pay the full cost of what it takes to deliver a product or service. And the workers who provide those products and services should be able to live off of their wages. Otherwise, it represents a transfer of value from those most in need to those least in need. In the end, a livable minimum wage would result in a more rational labor market and improved general allocation of America's resources of land, labor, and capital.

As someone who cut his teeth in retail, let me offer that buyers create markets, and sellers service them. And those serving markets are going to be successful only if they offer buyers a value proposition of either better quality at the same price, equal quality at a lower price, or a combination of the two. People are motivated to act in order to provide some product or service to a buyer who is willing to give them money for it. Buyers create markets. Sellers serve them.

Supply-side economics is a bunch of bunk. Building a widget factory doesn't create demand for widgets. Trick-down Economics is a bunch of bunk. You cannot point to a single example of its having worked. Yet some economists continue to sell it, and some politicians continue to buy it, because special interests love to pay low taxes on promises that it will stimulate the economy. But Trickle-down Economics simply doesn't work in practice. At least, it hasn't so far

Trickle-up is the proven path to a growing economy. If you pay people a living wage, they consume goods and services that require jobs to produce those goods or services. Those newly employed workers will need to buy more goods that have to be made. And so, the multiplier effect of job and economic growth propels job growth and the economy forward. Those who invest in and build businesses that serve the growing demand for products from a healthy workforce become winners—not by exploitation, but through offering people what they want to buy at a price that they can afford.

With that in mind, there are some very powerful benefits from a wage policy that offers a path out of poverty. Not only do individual wage earners get lifted up the economic ladder, as do their families; the communities they live in get lifted up as well. But there is an equally powerful cultural benefit that takes place, which is that America can once again advance toward a meritocracy, a place where all you have to do to make it in America is receive an education, public or private, find a job for which you are qualified, and work hard.

A lot of poverty, crime, and civil unrest can be linked, to some degree, to a lack of opportunity, equal or otherwise. The lack of equal access to education, jobs, and justice, represents a dark hole in the path to the American Dream. Equal opportunity for all is one of the greatest driving factors and motivators of human achievement that can propel America forward. Equal opportunity provides a pathway for more Americans to row our economic vessel in the same direction, where the benefits are shared mostly on an ability to contribute to the whole. It is the lack thereof that generates and fosters anger and resentment. Lack of equal opportunity doesn't cause all of our problems, but it plants the seeds for unrest.

It is a mistake that we don't teach capitalism in our high schools, so that the basic economic principles of supply and demand, capital formation, and entrepreneurism can be taught as productive civil forces. We do teach government, but not the economic system that drives government. A system with some level of government protections, like a livable wage, would motivate Americans to perform at the highest levels and achieve the most.

Now the question about the government being the employer of last resort at a fair minimum wage for bona fide U.S. citizen adults can be addressed. This program needs to be exempt from normal collective bargaining rights, because if you couple a livable minimum wage and a guaranteed government job, we greatly expose the country to having the government being the dominant employer, instead of a gateway to success. It's not meant to be comfort class, just the minimum necessary to be self-sustaining, without a pension, including social security. We want strong incentives for people to rise above a minimum-wage guaranteed-work-program job.

It is much better to pay people for working than to pay them for not working through all sorts of transfer payments like food stamps, housing assistance, and medical care through hospital emergency rooms, for example. People feel better about themselves if they are working and contributing to their own well-being and to the success of their community. Not requiring able-bodied individuals to contribute to their own welfare and well-being is a structural flaw in our socio-economic system that is not healthy for the person, and something we cannot afford to sustain financially as a society. If the choice is to pay someone for not working, versus working, then of course we should pay them for working. Let's not get too caught up in the wasteful government spending direction. Any actual work product is better than none, when compared to a handout instead of a helping hand.

The opportunity to work, along with a fair minimum wage, will most importantly help us change our culture to a more productive one. One less dependent upon transfer payments and entitlements, and one that rewards self-motivation and hard work. I believe it will do more to lift people out of poverty than anything that is being tried.

CHAPTER 5

THE HAVES AND HAVE-NOTS

America is still largely a land of opportunity, just not one of equal opportunity. Truth be told, it never really has been. But that doesn't mean we shouldn't aspire to be that place. History has shown that race, wealth, education, and pedigree are factors that have given many advantaged Americans a leg up over their neighbors. Many Americans' only chance for success is to be included in a meritocracy where your qualifications and work product determine your general level of financial success.

Even with the systemic advantages and disadvantages built into the system, America is still a beacon of hope for people from all over the world. Because of our rule of law, property, and legal and human rights, the United States continues to attract immigrants because they still view the U.S. as a land of opportunity, even with all of its challenges.

All that said, it is clear that the tilt in favor of the rich, is becoming steeper. There are a number of indicators for this, as well as reasons for it. The clearest evidence of this is that the concentration of wealth at the top has risen dramatically, so much so that 40% of the country's wealth is now owned by the top 1%. That is an astonishing number, up from an already very high number of 34.6% in 2007.

Another sign of the growing disparity of wealth and opportunity in America became evident during the last deep recession. In all post-World War II recessions prior to the one starting in 2008, corporate earnings suffered dramatically when unemployment rose above 6 or 7%, with many companies losing money. However, during the 2008-2009 recession, when unemployment rates hit 8%, corporate earnings were still positive and healthy on aggregate, instead of negative. Companies were able to do well because the percentage of those still working was still robust enough, in absolute terms, to generate enough consumer spendable wealth and consumer demand for companies to sell enough product to make healthy profits. Businesses did well, even though a large number of Americans were still suffering. In my fifty-year history of following the economy and the markets, this represented a watershed marker, because it illuminated the fact that the structural economic divide is so wide that we have two Americas: one where opportunity is locked in, and one where it is largely locked out. When your neighbor loses their job, it is a recession. When you lose your job, it is a depression.

A larger portion of Americans with means are economically disconnected from those who are suffering at the bottom of the economic ladder. This disconnection and disparity in wealth and lack of equal opportunity may be growing high enough to start causing enough resentment among the growing underclass to evolve into a form of class warfare. The Black Lives Matter movement is a symptom and a symbol of it. The popularity of populist candidates like Donald Trump on the right and Bernie Sanders on the left were reflective of people's exasperation with government's inability to be functional and fair. Our goal as a country should be to provide enough opportunity so that people don't feel hopeless, helpless, abused, or left out. They must feel they have a real opportunity to realize the American Dream, no matter where their family started on the economic ladder.

Most of us baby boomers know that our parents' generation could support a family with one working parent. Now, far too many families struggle even with both parents working. And for the first time in the American experience, our children will likely have less opportunity for success than the generation before them. We know that, and unfortunately, they know that as well. That too has a negative impact on the young American psyche. It seems un-American, even.

There are plenty of indicators that the rich are getting richer at the expense of the poor. Why has the disparity in wealth and opportunity grown over time, and what can we do about it?

In order to find solutions, we need to understand the problems. For most of human history, labor has been exploited. People were enslaved, served in serfdoms, were subjects of feudal warlords, and generally were conquered and raped, pillaged and plundered. The ruling class and bourgeoisie have almost always prospered at the expense of the proletariat, working class, or underprivileged. They had the land, the capital, and the weapons, while the masses had none.

With the advancement of religion and during periods of enlightenment like the Renaissance, educated peoples became concerned with the well-being of the common man. At times this realization came both out of compassion—and self-preservation, to be certain. Revolutions are most likely to happen because too many people are underserved by the governing elite. Both the French and American Revolution are testaments to that.

There were two major turning points in the development of a strong middle class in the United States. The first was the abolition of slavery as a result of the Civil War. We would have remained stuck in the Middle Ages had we not overcome the tragedy and suffering of slavery. The second major advancement was the development of labor unions, particularly the passage of the Wagner act in 1935, which established the National Labor Relations Board and institutionalized the protection of workers. It gave millions of workers collective bargaining rights for the first time.

A true and fair capitalist system requires a balance of rewards serving the contributions of land, labor, and capital in order for an enterprise to form. In order for a food crop to be produced, it takes land, of course, labor to till the soil, and capital, or money, for things like seed and fertilizer. Contributors of all three elements have to want to willingly make their contributions, un-coerced, believing the end product is a potential winner, for capital formation to be successful, and for exploitation to be avoided. Contributions made under duress are forms of exploitation.

The Wagner Act ushered in a fairer balance and share of the economic value pie across land, labor and capital. Unions are largely political organizations now with their own set of problems. But the important thing is that fair wages helped to build the middle class and changed our cultural view of the value of labor. The rich were still able to get richer, without leaving the working poor so far behind.

The Supreme Court decision in the 1954 Brown v Board of Education of Topeka civil rights case further helped level the playing field when it came to minorities, in stating that separate was not equal. The Civil Rights movement and the Voting Rights Acts of the 1960s further advanced the economic position of the non-rich. We were on our way, it seemed. So, what has happened to cause us to regress?

It starts with the concentration of political power in the hands of those with the money to influence elections—corporations and billionaires who often are able to expand their wealth through government contracts, licenses, and relationships, as a result of the access and relationships they buy. The level of access can also result in reduced regulations and favored tax breaks.

I'm a pragmatist who recognizes the reality that a money underbelly has always been a part of our political system and will likely continue to be unless we come up with a radically different way to pay for campaigns. But the growing disparity of financial wealth, I believe, is linked in part to the growing concentration of political power, financed more and more by the wealthy.

I believe that the next most significant factor in the growing disparity in wealth and opportunity is a result of the repeal of the Glass-Steagall Act. The Glass-Steagall Act usually refers to the four provisions of the U.S. Banking Act of 1933 that limited commercial bank securities activities and affiliations within commercial banks and securities firms.

One of the greatest strengths of America comes from the ability for one to be rewarded with the fruits of their own labors, manifested in the modern world largely through the commercial markets, including the capital markets. But as a caution, history has shown us that laissez-faire, hands-off economics on the part of the government doesn't serve the mass population and directly leads to concentrated wealth and power—and at times, even revolution.

At the dawn of the 20th century, trust-busting President Teddy Roosevelt, making use of the anti-monopoly Sherman Act passed in 1890, dismantled the Northern Securities Company. Roosevelt saw the company as little more than a vehicle for collusion and price fixing by America's railroad barons. This act by President Roosevelt was perhaps the country's first major act to truly try and level the working field between the wealthy class and the general population.

The Wagner and Glass-Steagall Acts were passed during the Great Depression. It took such desperate times for the masses, and such low demand for goods that the wealthy were selling, for Congress to act and move in a variety of meaningful ways to protect ordinary people from the power that concentrated wealth had achieved.

The Glass-Steagall Act helped establish a sound banking system to allow for commerce to take place on a stable basis. It ushered in the FDIC, the Federal Deposit Insurance Corporation, which insured bank deposits so that consumers didn't feel compelled to cause runs on banks out of fear of losing their money.

FDIC insurance was designed to help provide stability for banks, along with the housing market, not to underwrite commercial investment and lending risks. If a local bank made bad loans, the FDIC would intervene in the case of bankruptcy, in order to protect depositors. But the bank shareholders, usually including the bank president, lost all their money first, as a result of poor lending decisions. Even though the government became a backstop, the bankers had more to lose than the government.

The Act created savings banks that took in local deposits and loaned money primarily for home mortgages. They were allowed to pay depositors higher interest rates than commercial banks in order to help provide extra liquidity for home ownership, a cultural value. Fannie Mae and Freddie Mac were established to provide money for home ownership. It established intrastate banking that limited banks to operating only in their home states, instead of the interstate banking that was allowed some decades later. This in itself has turned out to be another contributor to wealth concentration.

The Glass-Steagall Act was an attempt to protect Americans from the core business models of the investment banking, brokerage, and insurance industries, where they get the often inexperienced customer to take on as much risk as they can sell them, with the financial services companies able to unfairly squeeze out an outsized portion of the profits

31

or rewards, often hidden to the investor. By getting customers to borrow money to take more risk, bankers, investment bankers, brokers and others, can make more money at other people's expense. But these institutions, too often, promote the purchase of investment products where the customers take risks that they either don't understand or which are not appropriate, while Wall Street gets guaranteed rewards in the form of fees and commissions. Wall Street is a treacherous place if one doesn't know what they are doing. I've learned that as a survivor of the treachery of the markets as a fiduciary Registered Investment Advisor for over twenty-five years. We need Wall Street. But we need it to be fair.

Once the Glass-Steagall Act was repealed in 1999, Sanford Weil, one of the architects and promoters of the idea, and a Wall Street titan already, sprang into action. He engineered what turned out to be the merger of Citibank, Travelers Insurance Company, and Smith Barney Investment Banking and Brokerage services, with Mr. Weil running the new behemoth financial services company. This was among the first of hundreds of consolidation transactions that took place across the financial services sector post Glass-Steagall.

What the repeal allowed for was the creation of bank holding companies that had merged insurance, banking, investment banking, and brokerage firms as subsidiary institutions. The banks took in deposits and made big and leveraged bets up their corporate hierarchy, on continued strong growth assumptions in the economy and the markets. Wall Street helped to hype up the already overheated housing market, lending money to all those who were eager to buy homes they often only wanted to flip for a quick profit. The banks made money on the lending, the transactions themselves, and the servicing of the loans, and they made money selling the questionable mortgages to unsuspecting investors.

The ability to enrich themselves at the cost of their customers was handed to these mega institutions on a silver platter, courtesy of the

Federal government, or rather the elected politicians who were apprecia-tive of the financial support they had received by the titans of Wall Street. And when the house of cards came down, the federal government was left holding the bag by being obligated to repay the depositors when the banks couldn't. New regulations that came into place after the financial collapse in 2008, that increased bank capital requirements sufficient to pass certain financial stress tests was a good step. But it is but a band-aide solution when it comes to the ultimate protection against Wall Street excesses.

I almost want to apologize for spending so much time on Glass-Steagall, but it was such a big mistake to repeal it. It has, and will con-tinue to have, a significant impact on the growing disparity of wealth, until we pass new legislation that repositions the balance between those who take risks and those who get the rewards. If we don't, current bank-ing laws will continue to undermine productive capital formation and economic growth in the U.S., and investors will further be harmed by an unfair investment playing field. Those who take risks should be re-warded commensurately with the value of their contributions to success-ful business enterprise. In other words, a meritocracy. A core foundation of American values.

CHAPTER 6

A TAXING PROPOSITION

We all know that our tax system needs massive restructuring. We tax gasoline, cigarettes, liquor, wages, dividends, and interest on our savings. We have a progressive income tax system that is supposed to require wealthy individuals pay at a higher rate than those less wealthy. We have inheritance taxes. We have taxes on corporations to make sure they and their shareholders help pay for the government that protects them from outside forces—a government that provides a safe and fair environment in which for them to compete. And we tax the gains on the sale of capital assets such as stocks, real estate, and other tangible holdings. These taxes, along with import duties, license fees, and other charges make up the vast majority of the revenues available to the federal government to pay its bills.

Even though these taxes were imposed with good intentions, it is clear to almost all that the system is not fair and it is way too complicated. It isn't fair because too many people of means and too many corporations don't pay their fair share due to special interest deductions allowed to them, the tax havens they enjoy, and the high-priced lawyers and accountants they hire to exploit all legal and questionably legal loopholes. Though our tax system isn't sufficient to capture a fair amount of taxes from the wealthy, it does however represent a full employment act for accountants and tax attorneys.

The rich are getting richer at the expense of the middle class. And we are saddling our children and grandchildren with massive debt that will stunt the growth of the economy and their own prosperity.

Before I offer some enhancements, let me suggest that the main goals of a tax system should be that it is fair, and that it is adequate to meet our fiscal needs. However, I don't agree that we need a balanced budget amendment. John Maynard Keynes, a key advisor to Franklin Roosevelt, opined and counseled that the government can afford periods of deficits during difficult economic times as long as it has surpluses during expansionary times. He has been incorrectly maligned for being the father of big deficits. He helped convince FDR to enact the work programs in the 1930s that helped save millions of American workers and helped put us on the path to recovery, even though it ballooned the federal deficit. Ultimately our recovery didn't really take hold until the government hired millions of Americans for our armies and factories during the Second World War. The money workers saved during the war also helped to fuel our economy once it ended.

A nation can always afford to pay some level of debt service as long as those payments don't amount to too big of a percentage of our Gross Domestic Product, which is approaching $20 trillion dollars a year. A huge advantage that the United States enjoys, unlike many other countries, is the fact that our population is growing, largely influenced by our traditional policies that attract ambitious immigrants. This means that the debts of past generations are paid for by a productive and growing working class.

Let me offer a different taxation paradigm. Let me first say that whatever we might do, it should <u>not</u> be implemented as an overnight replacement, but done incrementally to avoid shock waves to the economy.

The new paradigm I propose is to start taxing carbon-based energy on a consumptive basis in a much more material way than we do today with just a few cents of tax per gallon of gasoline. Instead we should increase the tax on gasoline by 10 cents a gallon for each of the next 10 years, until we reach $1 dollar per gallon. As we generate more from a gas tax, we match it with reductions in other taxes, principally personal income taxes.

I would normally be opposed to adding to sales taxes. A sales tax is a regressive tax that hurts the disadvantaged more than the advantaged. But we can largely offset the impact of rising fuel taxes by offering low-cost public transportation. What we gain is a way to get Americans off our addiction to oil-based energy, and help save the planet by releasing less CO2 into the atmosphere, a key cause of global warming. And we gain the ability to fund the development of non-carbon-based energy sources, perhaps funding the energy storage contest I suggested earlier.

We don't need a cumbersome and complicated value-added tax that taxes a product each step up the supply chain, but rather a simple Federal tax on carbon-based fuels. We should impose a higher tax on oil than for natural gas because of oil's larger carbon footprint. We could increase duties on imported oil in order to encourage domestic production, so that we utilize our own oil and gas resources on our path to a carbon-free energy footprint, instead of sending our money overseas.

I would start the taxing process incrementally. We can then see what revenue is produced, and reduce other taxes in concert along the way. In this way, there are no big jolts to the economy. Companies can position themselves over time to deal with an emerging tax regime that is predictable. We can make sure we have a better set of incentives in place to grow the economy on a path to a much cleaner planet.

In general, a progressive income tax system that taxes individuals with higher incomes at higher rates is fair because those more able to pay, pay more. On the other hand, we don't want the government to be confiscatory when it comes to taking too much of the fruits of the American worker's labor and risk taking. That works as a disincentive and undermines people's willingness to work hard and to risk capital.

We have local, state, and national taxes. Local government is typically funded through property taxes and sales taxes. State taxes come in the form of sales and income taxes. Federal taxes are mostly generated through the means already described. Whatever we do, it should be balanced in terms of the broad needs across our various forms of government.

I believe in a progressive tax structure, but one that is simplified. If we do the other measures offered in this book regarding guaranteed jobs, health care, social security, and the taxation of carbon-based fuels, then perhaps we could land at a place where personal income taxes can be cut dramatically, at least for middle-class and low-income Americans.

As for the wealthiest Americans, we can continue to ensure that much of the wealth they have produced can be passed on to future generations with a fairer federal estate tax. I would continue to exempt from inheritance tax a large enough amount that a family can pass on to the next generation, a successful family business, without having to incur perhaps significant debt in order to pay the tax and therefore hinder the business. The current family exemption is $11.58 million dollars. We can and should have a progressive inheritance tax that has those who are most able to pay, pay the most. Unlike all other forms of taxes, the inheritance tax is the only tax that can hold back the enormous advantage the ultra-rich having in compounding their wealth too often at the expense of the middle class. We can think of the inheritance tax as a very effective way to recycle excesses amounts of wealth generated in a generation, back to where it was harvested from: the Have-Nots.

Having a modest number of brackets in something like the following manner could represent a balanced approach where everyone is a winner. The entrepreneur still has the opportunity to serve markets sufficient to amass millions and even hundreds of billions of dollars in personal wealth, keep massive estates within a family, and help pay for the success of all of our citizenry without giving up any luxuries. With that in mind, perhaps the following schedule could be a good starting point for a constructive political discussion:

1. Exempt the first $10,000,000 estate and gift transfers from any inheritance taxes.
2. Tax any amounts above $10,000,000 up until $25,000,000 at 15%.
3. Tax any amounts above $25,000,000 up until $50,000,000 at 30%
4. Tax any amounts above $50,000,000 up until $100,000,000 at 40%.
5. And any amount above one hundred million might be taxed at 50%.

States also have inheritance taxes, so the highest rate would be somewhat higher than 50%.

This approach would allow the family farm to be passed from one generation to the other without the government taking it away or saddling the farm with debt to pay the taxes.

In the end, we will still need income taxes, corporate taxes, capital gains taxes, import duties, license fees, and such to help pay for the federal government. But in a more perfect Union, we can close the growing gap between the Haves and Have-Nots, and limit the loopholes that currently allow the wealthiest Americans to avoid paying their fair share.

CHAPTER 7

GETTING HEALTH CARE
OFF LIFE SUPPORT

I was hoping that the Affordable Care Act, otherwise known as Obamacare, was going to be that great stride forward in the advancement of the human condition, by increasing the availability, and affordability, for the general population to be covered by adequate health care. Eliminating the ability of insurance companies to reject coverage based upon pre-existing conditions was a huge victory. The Affordable Care Act (ACA) has survived threats to repeal it, and a decade after its creation is now supported by a majority of Americans. Still, we have a long way to go in order to provide something close to universal and affordable health care. The good news is that there are improvements being advanced and there is always hope that a bi-partisan approach can be found to improve the ACA, instead of derailing it and putting millions of Americans in jeopardy of losing their health care.

But I have to admit, I see material weaknesses and inadequacies in Obamacare—more regarding what it didn't accomplish, than what it did. To begin the discussion, let me suggest a simple set of national health care goals.

1. Continue to incentivize investments in high-risk private medical research through the promise of an opportunity for commensurately high profits. Every life-saving drug or advancement has to pay for nine unprofitable attempts, and therefore, things like price controls destroy the attractiveness of high-risk investments in medical technology. A Medicare for All mandate that includes government-controlled prices would be a capital formation killer in the area of medical advances.
2. Provide access to medical treatment to the general public at a price they can afford, so that major illnesses don't lead to financial collapse or bankruptcy.
3. Reward good behavior, not poor behavior. The insured who take care of their health should pay less for their health care on average than those who don't.

These are simple goals, but the path forward will take some explanation.

More medical innovation emanates from the United States than almost all the other countries combined. Why is that? Simply put, it's because investors are rewarded not just for the medical breakthroughs they finance, but also for the failures it took to get there. If they can't expect or hope to get a higher return than they can get from less risky endeavors, there is no reason for them to take those risks. Therefore, we don't want to limit the upside profit potential. The government should regulate efficacy and use, but not profits. Tax profits, but don't control or limit them. It is the Haves paying high prices for treatments, before others can afford it, that leads to the recouping of the research and development costs. In time, generic substitutes will lead to widespread consumer affordability, but we can't skip the originating step.

That means a drug company should be able to charge whatever the market will pay. If it wants to charge $1,000 per dosage for a limited, needed cure, then it should be free to do so as a way to recoup its costs. Charging a high price for a product that wouldn't exist without their risk-taking does no more harm to a person who can't afford the medicine than there would be if the medicine hadn't been invented in the first place. I understand this seems harsh. But it is a stark reality about how invention is funded in the private sector, from where 75% of U.S. medical research emanates. We want capital to flow to its highest and best reward. And we want the advancement of the human condition to continue to be a magnet for capital, and research.

Once inventors and patent-holders get their returns and are faced with patent expirations, then price competition comes into play. We all enjoy paying less for generic drugs than for branded ones, once those patents expire. The price of a twenty-year price monopoly is that we get the product in the first place, and a competitive environment in twenty years. Actually, companies usually have much less than twenty years to recover their research and development costs, and get a good return. That is because a patent, when achieved, is valid twenty years from the date of application, and not product introduction. It can take as much as ten years to get a product developed, through all approvals and produced in commercial quantities. The opportunity for high returns is what incentivizes the capital formation necessary for the invention of great commercial medical breakthroughs. It is up to the patent-holder to manage their own pricing over time. If an insurance company wants to negotiate a special volume price, as part of an insurance package, they have a right to do so.

Even though price fixing sounds attractive, it would lead to a slow-down in the development of life-saving drugs. The government does invest in research through the National Institute of Health, but at a fraction of the rate of Big Pharma. Universities are an important contributor to medical breakthroughs as well. But by far it is the private sector that invests the most in medical technology. More people in the future will benefit from future medical advancements, invented for the purpose of profit, than may be denied access today due to high prices for presently un-expired patented drugs. We don't want to extend the time it takes to invent an artificial eye, by decades, or even a hundred years, because we stifle risk-taking.

The wealthiest can afford first-class seats, the fanciest cars and the most expensive food before the general public, or mass market can. Their ability to pay high prices is a key catalyst for drug companies to make the very risky investments they do. Innovators with patents have less than twenty years of revenue and demand in order to maximize their returns. If they are successful, they will likely reinvest some of the profits into new advancements. This is part of the magic of the American capitalist system.

We currently have a patchwork domestic health care system. Today, in the first tier we have the private sector supported with private insurance. The second tier includes government-provided health care directly to patients, such as the VA and the Indian Health Services. The final tier includes Medicare and Medicaid, delivered through the private sector. The current collection of delivery systems isn't very efficient in terms of cost control, pricing, distribution, or availability. It also forces physicians to spend too much time away from direct patient care. This approach could be revamped in exchange for a hybrid approach that includes both a robust private sector and a public sector component.

I suggest we start with and maintain a full private healthcare system as the first tier. If you can afford to pay for the best medical care, you should be able to do so, either directly or through insurance coverage. This will continue to foster the level of innovation we enjoy today.

The second tier would be today's Medicaid and Medicare programs, where patient care is principally delivered by the private sector, or in the future, also through government-sponsored neighborhood healthcare clinics.

The third tier would provide healthcare for everybody else. The general U.S. citizen population not covered by private insurance, Medicare or Medicaid, could seek care from a nationwide government sponsored health clinic network, with payment based on ability, insured or otherwise. These neighborhood clinics could be administered and staffed by government medical staffs, or it could be out-sourced to the private sector.

Uninsured patients could either purchase insurance in the private sector or opt into a public insurance option, paying on a sliding scale, means tested, ability to pay basis. For working Americans, these premiums could be collected through payroll deductions like Social Security. At a minimum, this insurance would cover visits to the local neighborhood healthcare clinics. If you're unemployed, you might be required to pay a nominal $5-$10 for a visit. We would want to charge something, because the economics of zero pricing always leads to irrational allocations of limited resources. However, some accommodation would have to be made for the chronic indigent, at a lower cost than being treated in hospital emergency rooms, which for many today is their only option.

How would we accomplish this? We make it easier for young people to pursue their medical degrees. In return for a government-funded medical school scholarship, they would be required to practice in neighborhood health care facilities or surgical centers for a number of years. They would be paid a comfortable fair living wage salary but not be burdened with a crippling student loan debt and high medical malpractice insurance costs. When their term of service is completed, they would be free to pursue a higher salary in private practice. It is similar to the model currently practiced at the Cleveland Clinic. They pay doctors on salary, and not by the number of procedures or tests ordered, letting the doctors spend more time being doctors, than as for-profit, product delivery agents.

This approach has advantages for doctors and patients. It eliminates the practice of requiring unnecessary additional tests, which physicians often order to make more money or to protect themselves from a malpractice claim. Under the system I'm proposing, there would be no exposure to litigation. Instead of being able to sue, there would be effective internal quality control mechanisms in place to discipline and to weed out unqualified doctors. Demonstrated malpractice would lead to either decertification or even criminal action, in the worst cases. This would be a no-frills health care system that deals with 80% of human ailments, for 80+% of people's lives. There could even be a mental health component to it.

One of the biggest and obvious limitations of Obamacare is that it didn't introduce interstate healthcare insurance. Today, each state has its own licensing and set of regulations. Many states have too few participating insurance providers, thus reducing competition and keeping prices high. You should not have limited access to affordable insurance simply based on where you live. Interstate insurance markets would increase access to health care coverage and drive costs down through competition. We might wind up with ten to twenty mega nationwide insurance companies, or even regional carriers. Federal and state regulators would have to be alert to anti-competitive and unfair practices, but there should be costs savings when you can join an insurance pool larger than being restricted to your current state of residence. You would have more options and could pay for whatever level of service you want. You could get your primary care from the local government-run clinic if you wish, and purchase supplemental insurance for extra care in the private sector.

With today's technology, with just a fingerprint, or eyeball identification, all admission and payment information could be retrieved instantaneously before service is provided. Your medical records would follow you wherever you are treated so that almost all efforts are focused on medical care instead of administrative matters. Imagine that.

In this model, a twenty-year military veteran might have access to the neighborhood clinic, direct VA programs, and the private sector system through a voucher system, at little or no cost. Ten-year veterans may otherwise have to pay more for some of their care. Other first responders might also get special treatment in terms of access and co-pay costs.

Once we have provided affordable health care to all, we will need to consider the benefits of rewarding good behavior, and not bad behavior. The lifelong smoker shouldn't get a pass and expect the non-smoker to pay for the extra health costs associated with smoking. The insurance pool for smoking-related costs should be borne by smokers themselves through things like cigarette taxes and higher premiums. Likewise, we should be taxing sugar to help defray the cost of diabetes, heart disease, and other related health care costs, instead of giving billions away in federal sugar subsidies. Don't limit the size of sugared drinks, but rather, require the consumer pay the true costs.

Finally, we spend an inordinate amount of the nation's treasure on the last stages of a person's life. I read a book recently that I highly recommend. It is *Being Mortal: Medicine and What Matters in the End* by Dr. Atul Gawande. In it he describes a medical industry in which the primary goal is to extend life as long as possible, almost regardless of cost. He argues instead that we should be focusing on extending the time with a quality of life, sometimes at the expense of longevity. I believe we need to find a new culturally balanced approach to end of life health care. We should have a vibrant national dialogue.

Our health care system, which is still the envy of the world, and from which the most promising discoveries are made, still leaves too many people behind. It is inefficient and costs too much relative to what other medical programs in other countries can offer. Those countries benefit from the medical advancements invented in the U.S. and are also beneficiaries of lower prices than Americans pay. I am okay with that as a form of foreign aid, and as a way to expand the market for our medical achievements. It also increases the incentive for companies to make investments in medical technology.

The modified three-tiered approach presented here is intended to strengthen the Affordable Care Act, which was not quite the giant leap forward we were hoping for. And the Republican plan of just for-profit medical care will leave too many people behind. This approach will satisfy the three primary goals of maintaining a system that amply rewards medical breakthroughs, provides affordable access to basic medical care for all, and rewards good behavior, while attaching a cost to unhealthy behavior. I believe a more perfect Union can also be a healthier union.

CHAPTER 8

TAKING MENTAL
HEALTH SERIOUSLY

We all know of the importance of working to maintain our physical health. However, I know as a parent and an observer of life, that if children are physically well but suffer from mental health or emotional issues, they will suffer in school and in the working world. These issues can be caused by stress, poverty, and abuse, as well as biological and environmental factors. That is why we should make mental health check-ups available just like we do physical check-ups—perhaps at our local neighborhood government-run health clinics.

When I was young, most of society still considered those who suffered from mental health issues to be crazy, or bad, or someone to avoid. Often people would cross the street so they wouldn't have to come into eye contact with such a person. As a society we have come a long way in terms of our compassion for the mentally ill. As we do with traditional health care, we still have a long way to go.

Engaging mental health issues is part of my family heritage. I am very proud of my mother, Natalie Gottstein, who, in the 1980s, before she passed, was the Executive Director of the Alaska Mental Health Association. I am proud of her because she championed an historic cause in Alaska in advancing care for those people with special needs when it came to their emotional well-being. Before Alaska became our 49th State, Congress was sensitive to the fact that the new state would have modest resources in order to care for the mentally ill. So, it set aside a million acres of what was to become state lands, the economic benefits of which were to be dedicated to the care and treatment of the mentally ill. Unfortunately, over the next twenty-five years, the legislature, instead of using the land as intended, chose to siphon the money into the general fund, and spent it for other purposes.

In her capacity as the Executive Director of the Alaska Mental Health Association, my mother filed suit against the State, on behalf of the beneficiaries, for violating the State's legal obligations. Her efforts prevailed and she won $400 million dollars on behalf of the mentally ill. The money was used to establish and fund the Alaska State Mental Health Trust. To this day, the Trust is used to provide mental health assistance to those in need with afflictions such as alcoholism, schizophrenia, and other mental health disorders. For those people, most importantly, it has been a godsend. And for society, it has reduced drunk driving, crime, and the health care costs for thousands of people who otherwise would be much less functional, and more reliant on government services. Mental health services can and do help, if they are funded, administered, and delivered properly.

Everyone's body is different. And so is each person's mind. We all start out differently, and we grow from there. Some are blessed with superior bone structure and muscle mass, and others less so. And some come into the world without all the normal pieces and parts both physically and mentally, or without them all being connected properly. Throughout history, people who were different, and who acted differently, or who couldn't do normal things, were often cast aside by cultures either fearful of those who were different, or who lacked empathy and compassion.

I am sure there are more forms of mental illness than I can imagine. I'm not qualified to address the causes of even a fraction of them. But I don't believe we do enough for those who suffer emotionally or with mental illness and emotional stress. It causes problems for them. And it causes problems for society at large. Sandy Hook Elementary School, where twenty young children were murdered, along with six of their teachers, is a tragic consequence and symptom of problems not being identified early enough. Sandy Hook, Columbine, Stoneman Douglas; the list goes on, tragic reminders and markers of children with pain and needs that were not identified and treated, or isolated soon enough before they committed mass murder. We cannot save the world. And we cannot treat or cure everyone. But we can do a lot more, and we can do a lot better. I would go so far as to suggest that we bring counselors into our schools to provide mental health check-ups for students, so that we can detect and treat problems early on.

I think we all appreciate that even if every child grew up with two loving parents, in a safe neighborhood and environment, ripe with opportunity, that not all of them would be equipped to succeed. Some will still have brain function limitations, and/or emotional problems that are unavoidable to some degree or another. The question becomes, how do we identify the ones who need extra help, and help them in time? And if we identify a child with pathologically violent markers, what do we do if they haven't committed a crime? These are tough problems to solve and societal questions to answer.

I believe the answer is somewhere in a line to be drawn between parental rights and responsibilities, and the right and responsibility for government to be paternalistic itself in protecting children. We accept a responsibility to try and protect a child from sexual abuse. We protect them from diseases through vaccinations. But what about mental abuse that could contribute to mental illness and acts of violence, and poverty or neglect? When does the right of the community, acted upon by their government, supersede the right of a parent? It is a hard and complex set of questions that requires great caution, but we might aspire to have that dialogue.

In Israel, where almost all young Israelis are required to serve their country either in the military, or in the delivery of government social programs, young people, girls primarily, go into the homes of immigrant families and help them adapt to their new environment. It is considered a societal benefit and not an intrusion.

We might also consider a work-fare job corps that includes an army of household survey-takers who make assessments about primary needs being met for children. These visits would not be mandatory, unless some kind of government assistance is applied for, or evidence of abuse is present. These assessments could include investigations regarding nutritional needs, health care needs, school homework study deficiencies, and signs of abuse.

Annual health check-ups at the local government sponsored health care clinics could include mental health check-ups as well. I don't know what level of engagement, and in what form, makes the most sense. I do believe we need a discussion about what level of engagement is the right balance, in the hopes we can identify, help, or isolate those in need, before they become a danger to themselves and others.

If we do these things, we will help to keep relatively smaller problems from turning into bigger problems. It would hopefully lead to lower crime rates, lower amounts of welfare, and more economic productivity. And most importantly, it would provide an opportunity for a better quality of life for those less fortunate.

CHAPTER 9
SAVING SOCIAL SECURITY

When the Social Security System was implemented in the 1930s, the retirement age was sixty-five, while the average life expectancy was just sixty. The millions of people who worked and paid into the system, who unfortunately died before they could receive their retirement benefits, made it possible for the Social Security System to be solvent.

Unfortunately, our entitlement programs, particularly Social Security, are no longer sound from an actuarial point of view because people are living longer, the birth rate is declining, and benefits have risen through a series of generous cost of living adjustments. Up until 2013, the taxes from working Americans exceeded the benefits paid to retirees. But since then, Social Security has had to draw from general funds to make its promised payments to retirees.

The only substantial changes we can make are to increase the retirement age, reduce benefits, or raise Social Security taxes. Taking this into consideration, I would offer three structural enhancements that, if implemented, should materially improve the solvency level of our national retirement system:

1. **We should change the retirement age for new entrants into the program.** A formula based on retirement at the age of sixty-five

no longer works. We can and should raise the retirement age for anyone under the age of forty. I would scale it in the following way.

Current age below 25=Retirement age 70
Current age 25 to 29 = Retirement age 69
Current age 30 to 35 = Retirement age 68
Current age 36 to 39 = Retirement age 67
Current age 40+   = Retirement age 66

If we made these changes, we would dramatically improve the soundness of the retirement system and wouldn't impact anybody yet who is looking toward retirement. I don't know if the age of seventy is the right age to make the system sound. It might be seventy-two. It's a function of how many years and amount of contributions match the benefit obligations owed based upon average life expectancy, considerate of mortality rates, and any growing workforce.

2. **We can improve the relationship between contributions and benefits.** We want people to go through their working life with the confidence to know that if they contribute to the system, it will be there to distribute back to them a livable and affordable retirement. We should want it to be sound on an actuary basis with long-term pooled contributions by workers matching the amount of long-term pooled benefits. Expanded benefits would be justified only by a growing productive economy and a work-force able to underwrite any expansion. We would still maintain a defined benefit model, but one that balances benefits more di-rectly to contributions, a growing workforce or a change in mor-tality rates.

3. **Our benefit entitlements should be means-tested**. Individuals in higher earnings brackets might see their benefits curtailed,

limited, or fully taxed back. In other words, if an individual is worth $25 million or $50 million dollars or more, or some reasonable number, they might forfeit their Social Security benefits. If you believe that Social Security exists to provide security, and you have been fortunate enough in your working career to secure your own retirement, the monthly income provided by Social Security is likely negligible. If you don't need a safety net, you can make it stronger for your fellow Americans.

If we do these three things—make benefits tied more to contributions, means-test it, and modestly raise the retirement age—then we most likely will avoid a very huge problem in the next 30-50 years. As America's retirement population grows faster than a contributing workforce, we need real answers that rise above accounting gimmickry and political pandering.

CHAPTER 10

A UNION MORE PERFECT

In 1786, way before the 1935 Wagner Act, which guaranteed the right of workers to unionize, printers in Philadelphia struck for increased wages, and won. It represented a small but important event in the advancement of labor being valued. The next year the United States Constitution was adopted.

Throughout history, people of non-royal ancestry were considered expendable for reasons of territorial conquest and the accumulation of wealth and power. From the institution of slavery to the exploitation of child labor, it has only been about 150 years since America began, as a nation, to evolve beyond these dark human conditions. Therefore, the development of labor unions must be seen as an important advancement of human rights and Western civilization. The movement also initiated a cycle of reducing the disparity of wealth. But there is more to the story, and for me it is somewhat personal.

My grandfather started a grocery business out of a tent in Anchorage, Alaska, in 1915. As the city developed and grew, so did our family business. The American labor movement, and particularly the Teamsters Union, eventually found its way to Alaska. As my father told the story, my grandfather, a liberal and fair-minded person, didn't wait for the union to contact him. Instead he contacted the union, and signed up his small crew as members.

Over the decades as the business grew, it employed hundreds of Teamsters. My father taught me that it was good for us when the workers have fair representation. If the union did its job, we could call on it to provide us trained men and women to do the work we needed done. The union would work with us to discipline the poor workers and bad apples, so it could maintain a disciplined and work ready bench of qualified and productive workers. We were allowed to change our labor force needs on a weekly and daily basis, as market conditions dictated. As long as we didn't have to pay more than our competition, or at least could remain competitive, then we could work to earn our share of the grocery market, and provide good paying jobs for our employees. The grocery business is a very thin margin business. Any cost that gets out of control can cost you the business.

Things began to change after oil was discovered on the North Slope of Alaska in Prudhoe Bay in 1967. That led to the construction of the Trans Alaska Oil Pipeline in the mid-'70s, at the time, the single largest construction project ever attempted by the private sector. The Teamsters played a big role. Their job ranks ballooned from thousands to tens of thousands almost overnight.

It made the Teamster boss in Alaska very powerful—more powerful than the governor, most people thought. His name was Jesse Carr. He had been a labor business agent servicing my father's grocery warehouse in the 1950s. In order to better position his union, and his members, he established a hard-bargaining position that a Teamster was a Teamster, and should be paid the same regardless of the job asked to be done, regardless of the industry in which they worked. That forced Teamster wages across the state to rise to the amount being paid to workers building a massive and costly oil pipeline. For the grocery business, the requirement to pay our local warehousemen the high pipeline construction wages, instead of the same wages paid by our competitors in Seattle, plus a cost of living adjustment, was unsustainable. It made us uncompetitive. Even though we were selling more groceries, we were losing money.

In the end, the union settled for a two-tier workforce made up of regular Teamsters and part-timers. Our cost per hour for the regular and tenured Teamster was about $36 per hour, including benefits. This was all the way back in the mid-'80s. The part-timers were paid a third of what regular members made, at about $12 per hour, with few benefits. Had this compromise not been achieved, we would have remained uncompetitive and would have opened the door for us to go non-union.

In effect, the union's political organization created a class system within itself in order to get its voting rank and file workers to vote for them. The part-timers weren't allowed to vote, but they had to pay dues. It didn't seem fair to us, but that was a union issue. We were focused on how to remain competitive. Safeway, one of the largest grocery chains in the country, was our chief competitor. And their grocery warehouse was located in Washington State, with labor costs about 20% less than ours, even with the two-tiered wage system. We could justify the higher costs only by being able to offer better just-in-time delivery service to our customers as a result of having invested in a locally built and more costly distribution center.

That lesson, in part, taught me that labor unions are largely political organizations now, that serve the leadership first, the current workers second, and the future workers get left behind. In a labor leader's quest to get re-elected, he or she captures for their current constituents as much as he or she can get for them, even if it puts the union in a high cost long-term strategic cost disadvantage. By the time these agreements have priced union workers out of the market, the union boss has typically retired. That's what happened to the U.S. auto industry, the airline industry, and even the retail industry. The percentage of American workers belonging to a union is half of what it was fifty years ago, and continues to decline. Consider, Walmart is the largest retailer in the world and it isn't unionized.

It's not just pay but also work rules. The goal should be to produce goods and services as efficiently as possible, but in a manner that the consumer gets served first, because buyers create markets, and sellers serve them. Then, as long as workers get paid a fair day's wage for a fair day's work, and there is enough left over for the company to make enough profit to motivate them to continue to produce, then everybody wins. The business and job opportunity is stable as long as the company continues to make products that are in demand at a price that supports fair wages and provides sufficient returns on capital that the company has an incentive to grow the business, and employ more people.

All workers deserve a living wage and benefits and to be represented, if they choose to be, by a labor union. But unions, if they are to survive, must adopt the mantra of "global competitiveness." There must be a balance between the price for a good or service a customer is willing to pay and the cost of a unionized employee to make it. If it isn't enough to pay the worker enough for a living wage, then the product or service shouldn't be made, and manufacturing jobs may be lost. There might be less variety for consumers, but we maintain the integrity of a fair marketplace, and those who do produce the goods receive a living wage. And if the wage-earner makes more than a living wage, but it is too high to sustain the business, or doesn't provide for a reasonable profit, then the job, justifiably, will be at risk.

The alternative is to accept a model where workers are paid below a living wage. Many Walmart employees, for example, still require public assistance to make ends meet. But Walmart has, so far, aggressively squelched any efforts by its employees to unionize. I don't pre-judge as to whether a company is union or not, as long as employees are treated fairly in terms of pay and other benefits.

If unions don't go back to the values that were put in place when they were granted special labor rights, they will continue to decline. They must embrace the value of global competitiveness, even at the expense of some current jobs. Otherwise, they continue to operate in an environment where they eat their young, the future job-seekers. Land and building owners, labor, and capital contributors have to be rewarded sufficient for them all to come together in order to establish and maintain a profitable and sustainable enterprise. Smart companies today know they need to take care of their employees. Ones that don't, risk higher labor turnover, and the delivery of lower levels of service to their customers. And perhaps they deserve to have their employees organize, in order to level the playing field.

CHAPTER 11

A NEW VISION OF CRIME AND PUNISHMENT

I have served on multiple juries, and I marvel at the process and ideals we strive to achieve. Everybody is innocent until proven guilty beyond a reasonable doubt, as judged by a jury of one's peers. You have the right to face your accuser. You have Miranda rights. A trial is conducted under the rules of evidence and discovery. As Americans, we enjoy all these protections and much more. It is a long way from the world of lynch mobs and summary executions. But even though we are still the envy of the world in protecting individual rights, we are still somewhat in the Middle Ages, it seems, in our approach to dealing with criminals, incarceration, and rehabilitation.

We incarcerate far too many people, especially for minor, victimless crimes. We incarcerate far too many innocent people, especially people of color. And we put young adults, who are likely to be one-time offenders, in prison with hardened criminals, where the only way to survive is to become a hardened criminal themselves. The result is that the likelihood of these first-time offenders becoming repeat offenders increases dramatically once they are released.

This practice of mass incarceration is causing big problems not just for the offenders, but for their families, and the system itself. Those sentenced to prison often leave hungry mouths at home to feed, reinforcing a cycle of poverty and crime within a family. This is all compounded by the lack of jobs in the inner cities, where kids have nothing to do but hang out and get into trouble—especially young boys.

We have too many children born out of wedlock and living in single-parent households. Young mothers are all too often living from welfare check to welfare check. Too many of our youth grow up in a community with run-down schools, and too few jobs to go around, especially for teenagers. Turning a blind eye to the causes of criminality compounds the irresponsibility and tragedy of filling our prisons with an over-represented population of black and brown inmates.

The study and understanding of criminology can be overwhelming. I am not a criminologist. Maybe that means I am at more liberty to think outside of the box. The first thing I would recommend, as I have earlier, is to have the government be the employer of last resort at minimum wage, with a special category for teenagers. A companion program would provide wage assistance to employers who hire and train young people in troubled neighborhoods. This would help get kids off the streets and give them something to do. It would teach them a work ethic, and a skill.

Secondly, we should have at least four different corrections programs, two each for juveniles and two each for adults. Keep the violent criminals, rapists, killers, and hard-drug dealers away from inmates serving time for non-violent crimes. We should also spend more effort to rehabilitate the non-violent offenders, where we'll have more success.

Let's put the non-violent criminals to work, at a sub-minimum wage, working in concert with industry and government. As long as we are paying to house inmates, government could pay for real job training as an incentive to businesses located near the prisons. Inmates could make commercial products, not just license plates. And they could earn a wage that benefits everyone. A third of the wages could go to help pay for their incarceration, a third for a victims' fund, and a third that the inmate can spend for extras in prison, send home, or save and legally invest.

Imagine giving inmates a real fresh start, where they have lots to lose by engaging in more crime. Where they have picked up a work ethic hopefully, with pride, along the way. I would suggest tying an opportunity for parole to success in this area, so that freedom comes with the responsibility to not only stay out of trouble, but to contribute to oneself and society as a whole. Let's create opportunities out of problems, rather than admit failure. Instead of just warehousing human beings and forgetting about them, let's be just, fair, compassionate, but also realistic.

On the other side of the criminal justice system are the men and women we entrust to protect and serve us. Police officers have among the toughest jobs in America, next to the brave men and women of our all-volunteer military. Our men and women in uniform protect us from outside forces, while the police protect us from bad forces from within. It is an important job to be a good police officer. It's a calling we want our young men and women to aspire to, if they have the courage, dedication, and strength of character enough to protect us and themselves as well.

The vast majority of police officers who serve with pride, and in the pursuit of equal justice for all, deserve our respect and heartfelt gratitude. But we should all recognize that police officers are people too, complete with all the weaknesses and flaws of any other human. I am sure that almost no police cadet enters a police academy to do bad things once they get a badge. But I have often wondered how a career exposed almost daily to the worst of the human condition could not help but have a negative impact on the best of us. Dealing with sexual assault, murder, and suicides takes a toll. Some become insulated emotionally just in order to survive. And some don't survive. In 2019, a police officer was more than twice as likely to take their own life than be killed in the line of duty.

Some police officers suffer from the same kind of post-traumatic stress disorder, or PTSD, that many of our soldiers bring home from the battlefield. Others develop prejudice that all too often manifests itself in mistreatment and brutality against the very citizens they are sworn to protect.

Today we are witnessing more and more examples of police brutality. Is this new? I don't think so. With millions of cellphones in the hands of our citizenry, video is captured and published, almost in real time. We're witnessing police conduct in a way we never have before. Many officers now wear body cameras, which can tell a more complete story, or all too often, confirm our worst suspicions.

George Floyd and Jacob Blake are just two of the most recent and highly publicized examples of police using deadly force. Floyd's death may have been the catalyst for the Black Lives Matter movement, but for black Americans, the circumstances of his death did not come as a surprise. How can that be acceptable in America? And how can we not do something about it?

We can start by incorporating sophisticated police hiring techniques that better identify prejudice and racist tendencies, weeding out potential problems in advance. Psychological profiles at the hiring stage are common practice at many police departments, but they are either flawed, or should be re-administered on a regular basis. We can also insist that police officers receive ongoing training on the use of excessive force.

Examples of police misconduct should be compiled in a national database and searchable by the public. A *USA Today* investigation found 85,000 cases of police misconduct in 2019 and published them. Such a database could help communities identify potential problem officers, and keep police departments from hiring them. But as *USA Today* reported, too often police unions have worked hard to shield those records from public view and have even had them destroyed. Congress is also considering abolishing or at least re-defining the concept of qualified immunity for police officers, which has been used to shield them from personal liability in police brutality cases. If the rest of us are responsible for the bad decisions we make on the job, why shouldn't police officers be held to the same standard, especially in cases of excessive force, where they are clearly in violation of their training?

In the end, even if we could weed out all of the prejudice and racism, there will be police officers who break bad. They drift too far down the slope of vice and easy money that they see every day. They might convince themselves, in justifying their actions, that their conduct isn't so bad, compared with what is going on around them. But of course, it is bad. It has victims and causes a breakdown of community trust, fear of police, and a sense that if the bright side can't protect you, then going to the dark side might be safer.

So, we have a high incarceration rate with its roots in a lack of equal opportunity, education, and jobs, and a policing industry that is on the defensive for being too complicit in unequal justice, and for not properly policing their own.

What might we do to turn things around? As an ordinary citizen, I would offer five suggestions. The first is the most important, and that is to provide a meritocracy where honest hard work can be counted on to be rewarded, where regardless of where one starts, there is an equal and fair opportunity for a good education, access to health care, and opportunities for jobs. There is a direct correlation, I believe, between lack of inherent and systemic opportunity and higher levels of poverty and crime. Minimum-wage employment of last resort might greatly reduce the crime rate and our prison populations, not to mention the $80 billion we spend every year in this country keeping people behind bars.

The second suggestion would be to adopt the framework of the progressive corrections programs I referred to earlier. Give the non-violent inmates the responsibility to develop self-pride through paid work, and the opportunity to develop skills for success in the outside world.

The third idea would be to provide real mental health resources in prisons. We have to be more holistic if we are going to be successful in reducing the number of repeat offenders. We have to understand a person and help them understand themselves in order to help them. I am sure there is a large percentage of inmates that we can't help. But there are many we can.

The fourth suggestion would be to give police officers a chance to care for their own mental health. We should recognize that policing, by its very nature, can wear a good person down, so just taking vacations every year isn't enough. I don't know what the correct number or ratio might be, but I would suggest, for example, that for every four to six months that an officer is on the front lines, they get a month of mental health stress relief. They can do what they want with the time, but should use it to reconnect with life outside the job, with full access to qualified counseling. We give our teachers a three-month mental health break every year. A police officer might need the same.

The fifth idea is that for those very few cases where corruption or criminal injustices are committed by officers, that a special prosecutor's office, enforcement, and court system be developed. This would go beyond what a traditional Internal Affairs department offers. It is important that the district attorneys and the police investigators who work together every day don't wind up in direct conflict with each other. There needs to be complete independence for prosecutors, and a safe way for good officers to report the bad conduct of bad officers.

These ideas alone won't solve the problem. But I think they might be a step in the right direction so that all Americans can have more confidence in our criminal justice system, and so that the vast majority of the fine men and woman who put a badge on every day don't get cast with the few bad apples in a very large barrel. We need to give our police departments the resources they need to protect us from our socio-economic failures, but we also have a responsibility to address those failures at the same time.

CHAPTER 12

A COUNTRY OF IMMIGRANTS

Like most Americans, I have a view about immigration, a view I believe I share with many of my fellow Americans. I don't like the idea that for decades we have allowed a somewhat porous border that has permitted millions of immigrants to enter our country illegally. I don't like the idea that many of these illegal immigrants take some jobs from Americans and those who reside legally. Their presence also places a financial burden in terms of government assistance, from education and healthcare, to law enforcement and prisons.

On the other hand, there are millions of jobs that Americans don't want to do that have long been relegated to immigrants, legal or otherwise. How many times have you heard of the story of the foreign single mother working two or more jobs cleaning houses so that she can feed her children and hopefully provide them access to the American education system and a path to prosperity? Or the immigrant farm worker from Mexico who toils in our fields doing back-breaking work in the hot sun in order to feed themselves and send a few dollars home? We should not think of these hard-working people as liabilities, but instead as assets.

I believe in a path to a legal status. If a person has broken no serious laws other than coming across the border illegally, has a job, is paying taxes, and can otherwise be shown to be a constructive member of society, then let's figure out a way for them to stay. However, we should do this commensurate with devising and implementing proper border security, coupled with a humane process of dealing with the challenges brought to our doorstep as a result of human migration, whether immigrants are seeking asylum or opportunity.

However, if on a path to legal status, an illegal alien commits a crime greater than a misdemeanor, they're gone. If they don't file an application for legal status, they're gone. If they don't pay their taxes, they're gone. That would set an important tone. There is a misperception planted and promoted in conservative circles that illegal immigrants are responsible for an increase in violent crime and property theft. But study after study has shown that the exact opposite is true. And if you think about that, it makes sense. Illegal immigrants are incentivized to be law-abiding, because if they are convicted, or even arrested on suspicion of violating our laws, they face prison time, deportation, or both.

If we establish a timeframe, such as ten years of constructive participation in society, then we should consider issuing a permanent work visa, and from there a path to citizenship. America benefits from the labor of millions of hard-working and honest Mexicans and other foreigners willing and able to do the work that almost no Americans want to do. Most of us are happy to have them do those jobs. I've yet to see an anti-immigration critic step forward and demand to clean houses, do yard work, or pick vegetables for minimum wage or less. The work of these immigrants contributes to our country's prosperity in the same way that a strong currency lowers the cost of living.

We are a country of immigrants. Unless you are Native American, someone in your family arrived on our shores as an immigrant. They did not shut the door behind themselves, and neither should we.

And finally, a word about the wall. It only takes a 21-foot ladder to get over a 20-foot wall. It simply won't stop human migration patterns that are a part of human history. I am not encouraging illegal immigration, but recognizing that as long as there is more opportunity here than in their home country, people will risk almost everything at a chance for a better life for themselves and their families. They always have. They always will. I would rather build an interstate water system than a wall with Mexico.

CHAPTER 13

LET'S GET GLOBAL

The word "globalization" almost seems like a dirty word to many people. At its core, globalization is the world's economies working collaboratively and competitively across borders to expand each country's global markets for their goods and services. It does so in a way that provides the greatest value of quality and price to more consumers around the world, as a function of local economic competitive advantages.

Globalization's natural economic forces mean success comes for suppliers by being able to provide consumers of goods and services around the world, the lowest prices, across the widest array of products possible. It represents, in the developed and developing world, a significant improvement in the quality of life of people. With lower trade barriers, each country or region can hopefully create at least one product or service it can offer to its region that's of better value and quality than the next-best competition. That is much easier said than done. Unfortunately, globalization hasn't yet gotten us to a commercial world without exploitation and unfair business practices. Child labor is rampant in Southeast Asia, and China manipulates its currency and steals patents, giving them an unfair advantage.

In order to deal with child labor practices, we should target those firms in violation and add tariffs in an amount greater than the amount of savings a company is enjoying by hiring under-aged workers. It must be made costlier to hire children than to pay adults a living wage. I would suggest that products coming into the country could have a human rights rating, allowing consumers the choice of avoiding products where labor and child exploitation takes place.

Historically, people have lived in one of two economic survival models. The first is characterized by a family with sufficient acreage of fertile farmland to provide enough food for the family, while having enough left over to sell to others to get whatever else they might need. There are no banks or currency required in this economic model. Barter systems have been in place and working for thousands of years. Salt became an early form of currency, and then later gold and silver when commerce began to expand beyond local markets.

The second model is represented by the majority of the world's population that doesn't own any farmland. People either work on somebody else's farm, or they are employed in some other job, where they are paid for their time. In this model, the question from a currency exchange and purchasing power parity point of view is how many hours of work does it take to buy food, clothing, and shelter? That is what determines a base form of purchasing power and purchasing power parity. Let's imagine we have two countries—Country A and Country B—neighboring each other, where workers in each country must work an hour getting paid a dollar an hour in order to buy a dozen eggs. That would represent purchasing power parity.

In a perfect world, each country would be the low-cost producer of a product in demand all over the world. But that world exists only in fairy tales. What we want is a fair trade and level playing field world where peoples and countries are encouraged, and educated, such that they become the low-cost provider in their region of a product or service, in order to gain the foreign currency needed to buy products from other countries. Cotton from Egypt goes around the world. As do automobiles from Germany.

There are a number of organizations, both governmental, like the World Bank, and the International Monetary Fund, and charitable organizations like the Bill and Melinda Gates Foundation, and the Ford Foundation, that work to advance better living conditions in less-advantaged countries. But clearly, much more work has to be done in order to advance working and living conditions for the greatest number of people around the world. And that is aside from all the global conflicts that are taking place, particularly in the Middle East and Africa.

Some of the negative commentary about globalization stems from the observation that we have fewer local owners of grocery and hardware stores, with profits staying in the community. Instead, we have lower prices on many of the things we buy at Walmart, Home Depot, or Lowes, resulting in enhanced purchasing power. Those who own shares in the national retailers benefit in the form of stock prices and dividends, whether they are local or not. It's a different world.

Globalization represents more of an opportunity than a cost, it seems to me. Countries that trade together are less likely to kill each other. The European Union was formed in part to generate common interests amongst the European countries. Europe hasn't been at war with itself since World War II.

For those who complain that globalization costs jobs, it is true for those who don't maintain an ability, through extra training and other forms of economical and rational investments, to be competitive on a regional or global basis. Many of those who complain, most likely are benefiting from the lower cost of goods that they purchase. They can't avoid it. Even if one buys a car from a domestic manufacturer, you are benefiting from lower prices resulting from foreign imports forcing local producers to be more competitive. And there are likely to be lower-cost foreign-produced parts in your vehicle as well. General Motors, its workers, shareholders, and consumers of their products, are benefiting from a new post-bankruptcy world because the enterprise has been better rationalized across the inputs of land, labor, and capital. Auto workers getting paid less is better than not getting paid. But their wages need and deserve to be at a living wage, commensurate with their job skills and productivity.

When we insert the economic forces of currency, debt, and interest rates across borders, we complicate things. For example, if the fiscal or monetary policies of a government lead to a significant increase in inflation, then it costs more in hours to buy the same amount of imported goods as before, if wage inflation doesn't keep up with general inflation, which it usually doesn't. It would take more hours of work to buy the same number of imported apples.

Inflated import prices naturally cause less demand for imported products. This results in less demand to convert the local currency into the foreign currency of the exporter to pay for those goods. This causes downward pricing pressure on the foreign currency relative to the local currency. The best way for a country to have and maintain a strong currency, which keeps the costs of imported items lower, and increases the purchasing power of its residents, is to have an educated and productive workforce, and not to accumulate too many deficits and too much debt.

Inflation causes a devaluation in the currency markets for the inflated economy. Any drop in the value of currency makes it more expensive to buy foreign goods. That adds to more inflation. On the other hand, it also makes domestically produced goods cost less relatively in terms of the foreign currency markets, because as a domestic currency drops in value, it makes the sale of domestically produced goods more competitive in the world markets. High inflation in any country can have serious consequences for its trading position in the world, relative to the inflation rate of its trading partners.

The price of debt, or the interest rate charged, also impacts cross-border transactions. In a rational bond or debt market, lenders compete for the best-quality borrowers. They also want the highest interest rate that can be charged and earned from the borrower. Typically, the longer the term of the loan, the higher the interest rate paid by the borrower. This is commonly referred to as the yield curve. Sometimes the yield curve gets inverted, and long-term rates are lower than intermediate-term rates, for example. Sometimes the slope is steep and sometimes it's flat, depending on regional and global economic conditions. There is even a new global phenomenon of negative interest rates.

I believe the yield curve, when it has abnormal shapes and metrics, represents a prism through which economic imbalances get rebalanced over time. It influences the flow of capital. Rising inflation and interest rates rewards those who had extra amounts of cash or short-term debt instruments providing resources available for investing. And it punishes those who purchased long- maturity bonds.

Inflation allows governments to pay back long-term debt with cheaper dollars. Rising inflation can be viewed as a purchasing power tax from which governments can benefit. Politicians get blamed less for inflation than for taxes. But inflation can represent a future, post-election societal burden as a consequence of pork barrel politics. Pork barrel politics directly adds to inflation. Spending the public's money unproductively makes us all poorer. A few ways that can be manifested in the economy is through higher inflation, higher interest rates, and a lower currency value. More people may have jobs due to government spending, but the pay for those jobs in purchasing power parity may erode. Americans have experienced this erosion over the last fifty years. Today, households may have more "things," but chances are it takes two working parents to pay for a family's needs, as opposed to days gone by when one worker, usually the husband, was able to pay the bills. One may not be in a lesser economic position, but are certainly poorer in terms of what is highly valuable: time.

All of these things influence purchasing power parity, levels of competitiveness around the world, and ultimately the standard of living of billions of people. I have to believe we are all better off when the greatest amount of people in the world have the opportunity to participate successfully in the global economy. The result of a more productive and fair work force around the world is that more people get to buy more goods for fewer hours worked, and thus are able to enjoy a higher quality of life. In the end, we all have more incentive to cooperate with each other economically, and fewer reasons for military conflict. I vote for fair trade and globalization.

CHAPTER 14

America's Place in the World

America has a unique role in world politics and influence unprecedented in world history. The Broken Window Theory postulates that a broken window left unrepaired invites more broken windows and the further deterioration of a neighborhood.

Many in the foreign policy arena describe America's role as repairing the broken glass in the important neighborhoods of our friends and allies. After the American soldier helped defeat the Axis powers in the Second World War, the world that remained was in shambles. Fifty million people were killed. Whole governments collapsed. The Marshall Plan was implemented, which advanced billions of dollars in aid so that Europe could rebuild. General Douglas MacArthur was tasked with setting up a new government in Japan. Institutions, including the United Nations, the International Monetary Fund, the World Bank, and NATO, were established so that when parts of the world faced challenges they couldn't meet alone, that the U.S. and our allies would step in to help restore stability, to repair the broken glass and prevent more broken windows from spreading to other neighborhoods. Without America's leadership and guiding principles in solving these global issues, a vacuum is created that our adversaries and competitors are quick to fill.

This doesn't mean that the U.S. has to be the world's policeman and force peace, security, and humanism around the world. We are powerful, but not that powerful. However, we do have an important role in helping to make sure that, within limits, we step in and make a difference. When the Soviet Union set a blockade around West Berlin in 1948, the U.S. organized the Berlin Airlift, flying in food, water, and medicine to the beleaguered city. Had America not done so, West Germany eventually may have succumbed to the Soviet threat, instead of surviving to be reunified with East Germany in 1989, once again becoming one Germany and a strong NATO ally.

Prior to the First World War, the U.S. was content to be isolationist, and foreign affairs were seen as precisely that. But we came to Europe's defense in 1917, and we prevailed. After the "war to end all wars," we again retreated from global activism. Even as the Nazis stormed across Europe and bombed London nightly, America kept its powder dry, much to the consternation of Sir Winston Churchill. But that ended after the attack on Pearl Harbor on December 7th, 1941, in what President Roosevelt called "A Day That Will Live in Infamy."

Since the Second World War, both political parties have supported the importance of American participation on an international scale. Our foreign aid programs represent less than 1% of our national budget, but they have played a vital role in helping to repair broken glass around the world, and keeping rocks from hitting our windows. America is a leader in providing food, medicine, and economic and military aid where they are most needed.

For example, today, the U.S. still provides the government of Lebanon with military assistance even though the country is controlled in large measure by the Hezbollah, a terrorist organization that is a direct threat to Israel and the West. We do so in order to maintain a seat at the table. Without our presence, Iran, Russia, and Turkey would have an opportunity to have greater influence in ways that could threaten our national security.

In recent years the U.S. has increasingly turned away from these global partnerships and has become more nationalistic. Invoking an "America First" ideology, we withdrew from the Paris Climate accord, the Trans Pacific Partnership Agreement, and even the World Health Organization. These withdrawals, along with vitriolic attacks and tariff battles with our allies, succeeded in further isolating America from the world and opening the door for a lot of broken glass to come.

It must be also remembered that even though there is adequate reason for the U.S. to re-establish its traditional leadership role on humanitarian grounds, it is also a national security imperative that we play an important role around the world. Our adversaries in the form of Russia, China, and Iran, are already filling the void and replacing our influence. This doesn't make us more secure, but rather puts us at greater risk. Consider what happened in Syria, where we abandoned our Kurdish allies who fought on our behalf in the war on terror, leaving them at the mercy of Turkish forces. That betrayal drove them into the arms of Russia and Iran.

Here then are three of our key foreign policy challenges, and how I believe we should address them, turning the threats to our union into opportunities.

China

When I was growing up, I remember hearing the phrase "East is East and West is West, and Never the Twain Shall Meet." It was a reference to the fact that our worlds are so different that we could never really have a good relationship. As a kid, I believed it, though I didn't really understand why it had to be so. When President Nixon went to China in 1972, it was an historic opening of a door. Then Deng Xiaoping, the Chairman of the Communist Party of China, opened the doors within China to private ownership and international trade in the 1980s, as part of the post-Mao China Revolution. It ignited, after decades of dormancy, growth of the Chinese economy and power at a revolutionary pace, which continues today.

After decades of rapid economic growth, market manipulations, theft of intellectual property, and a great build-up of their military capability, China has become our greatest competitor and potential adversary in the 21st century. China achieved all this while buying hundreds of billions of dollars of US debt that represents a substantial future call on assets tied to the American economy.

The massive trade deficit that has accumulated over the decades has three primary impacts. The first is that Americans have been able to purchase imports cheaper than they have been able to buy from U.S. manufacturers, adding to our purchasing power, and standard of living. However, the consequence is that China now owns over a trillion dollars of U.S. government debt, and Chinese companies have large investments on American soil. This represents a perpetual transfer of American wealth to China, as well as an influence on our interest rates, because if China stops purchasing U.S. debt, lessening demand, it could lower the price of our bonds, and increase interest rates.

Our relationship with China is now tightly tied together economically, but not culturally. And regardless of how much economic pressure we try to exert in correcting unfair trade practices, it is a very tall order to get China to reverse course in terms of the treatment of its people, or its aggressive actions toward Hong Kong, Taiwan, and in the South China Sea.

The cultural and political differences between America and China are tied to our histories. The foundation of China's governing principle—what is good for the whole is good for the individual—extends back through its history of dynasties and emperors. It created a largely submissive and obedient culture and population. That's in contrast to Western values that ascribe to the view that what is good for the individual is good for the whole. There is no Bill of Rights in China. It is contrary to their whole way of thinking. It gives them carte blanche to treat their people any way the Communist Party wishes to, in order to maintain authority and control, which is good and necessary for the people. The end justifies the means in Communist China-World.

That "good for the whole" mentality is what will force the Chinese government to squelch, over time, any dissent in Hong Kong, and eventually Taiwan. China cannot afford to let any dissent have any level of success, as it might embolden dissent across the country. At least, that is their belief.

China is also building man-made islands in the South China Sea, claiming sovereignty over the new territory, expanding its regional influence, while also gaining access to offshore oil and gas reservoirs. They have built one island that can land large military aircraft and house a permanent military base. In addition, they are quickly building up their naval operations, including aircraft carriers, such that it threatens the military pre-eminence in the region that the U.S. has enjoyed since the Second World War. China's actions make our Asian allies more vulnerable by threatening our ability to protect international shipping.

The signature long-term strategic foreign policy goal of China's current President Xi Jinping is what is often referred to as the Belt and Road Initiative, or sometimes as the New Silk Road. It is a highly sophisticated and ambitious effort to advance China's influence around the world in three key pillars.

The first pillar is the land pillar, the goal of which is to establish rail, pipeline, and other trans-national paths enabling China to send and receive products. The second pillar is of the sea, by establishing key port access around the region and the world, where it is deemed strategic. And the third pillar is in technology, from cyber to artificial intelligence. China wants other countries to adopt its technology and potentially become a hostage to it. The Chinese telecom company Huawei is exporting its next-generation communication technology around the world. The U.S. government warns that China can use Huawei's tech to steal corporate secrets, censor online content, and even track dissidents.

China uses its significant resources to bid on and finance large infrastructure projects around the world, including ports and pipelines, in order to gain influence, particularly when the benefiting country has trouble paying its debts. China is finding this kind of economic diplomacy can be as effective in protecting its global influence as much as foreign expansion. For example, Oman sells 86% of its oil exports to China, and Oman doesn't criticize China for how it treats its Muslim population. And by the way, China doesn't look at Hong Kong and Taiwan as opportunities for expansion, but as nothing more than a re-securing of its historical geographical footprint and borders.

China wants to diminish the stature of the United States on the world stage, relative to itself. But it still wants to use our strength. If the U.S. uses its resources to maintain stability in the Middle East, that is okay with China. It wants the Straits of Hormuz to stay open. China also wants to keep the peace with Iran, though it doesn't import any major oil quantities from there, so as not to offend the West. It wants to dethrone the U.S. as the only superpower, but not replace us. It looks to be everybody's friend, but not an ally. It won't come to any other country's military defense. It will say nice things about Iran while becoming a major trading partner with Israel.

While we are rightfully concerned over China's influence on North Korea, we must also recognize that the rogue nation represents a double-edged sword for China. On one hand, North Korea represents a geographic barrier separating the China from the West, represented by South Korea. On the other hand, China doesn't want millions of North Koreans pouring across its border escaping war, famine, or human rights abuses. As long as this balance is maintained, China appears willing to put up with a lot of North Korea's behavior and provide them economic assistance.

All this suggests four things. The first is that we will never materially influence China when it comes to human rights, unless we make it in the leadership's best interest in doing so. The second is that China, in the 21st century, represents a much bigger and growing military threat to us than Russia does, and there is nothing that we can do to stop it. However, we can advance our ability to compete with it. The third is that America will have to innovate and adapt commercially and militarily at an accelerating pace in order to continue to compete with China on the world stage. If we can't, it's our fault, not theirs. And fourth, only if we satisfy both China's and North Korea's security concerns will it be in both China's and North Korea's interests to have a nuclear-free Korean Peninsula.

So, what should our foreign policy be? I have a few ideas. The first is that we need to have a public dialogue as to whether or not the U.S. will stand behind its commitments to protect Taiwan from Communist Chinese rule. That would take making sure that Taiwan has an adequate military arsenal, along with a commitment to maintain a strong U.S. naval presence in a defensive posture. So far, we've been sending mixed signals, with actions that indicate we are willing to let Taiwan fall to Mainland China. I don't have a judgement here in terms of a solution, just a description of the forces and choices at play. My expectation is that Taiwan will eventually lose its independence, as Hong Kong already has. It might just take a hundred years.

I would not use a trade war and tariffs in order to correct the trade imbalances and intellectual property and technology thefts. It's too much like a circular firing squad. Everybody gets hurt. There are no winners. A better approach might be to assemble a set of pressures that could be increased incrementally and predictably over time, if the trade deficits don't improve over time. Put the burden on China to decide what mechanisms they put in place in order to reduce the trade deficit. To be successful, we have to make the cost of ignoring unfair trade practices costlier than addressing them, in a way that minimizes any self-inflicted economic wounds. We also need to recognize that China's economy is no longer growing purely as a result of exports. They have been so successful in growing their economy, and building their middle class, that they now produce more for domestic consumption than for export. That reduces our importance to them in terms of their economic vitality and dependency.

A trade deficit that is a result of our own inability to compete under fair-trading practices is our own fault. But China's currency manipulation, export subsidies, import restrictions, and intellectual property theft all fall outside fair-trading practices. Here then are some novel ideas to put in our trade toolbox when it comes to managing a new relationship with China.

1. We could set targets for China to reduce the trade deficit over time. And if those targets are not met, we could then impose any number of sanctions, including import restrictions and non-discriminatory tariffs. This would reduce import demand and cause economic pain to China that they would have to consider in the calculus of their behavior. This lets the Chinese figure out how best to get there over time from their own domestic policy point of view, without creating a crisis. We need to find the balance whereby unfair trade practices result in fewer jobs for China, not more, and where not engaging is costlier than playing ball.

2. When it comes to intellectual property, it isn't realistic to expect the Chinese to enforce our patent laws and rights. But what we can do, working with our European and Asian partners, is to embargo Chinese companies that are proven to have products that violate Western patents. It will mean that China will be able to continue to steal technology and use it domestically, but it will cost them in foreign markets. So, if the additional profit made by selling fully in the global markets would exceed the savings by stealing intellectual property, then the Chinese would be economically motivated to be more innovative and less duplicative. We can hopefully make stealing patents too costly a business expense.

3. Give China an opportunity to offset the penalties for unfair trade practices in exchange for success in getting North Korea to curtail or abandon its nuclear ambitions. This would have to be coupled with security guarantees and substantial economic aid going to North Korea.

4. I would require any product entering the U.S. carry a rating that would allow consumers to decide if they want to purchase a product where human exploitation is involved. Instead of product ingredients, it would be a human rights table. Any foreign company doing a large amount of business in the U.S. would be required to pay to have their plants independently inspected and investigated as to whether they have exploitive labor practices, child and otherwise, along with safety issues. Ideally, this could be done on an international scale through the World Trade Organization or United Nations. But even if the U.S. stands alone in this, it could have a positive impact on working conditions globally.

5. As a last resort, if China's economic and military belligerence gets too severe, we could suspend interest payments on the U.S. debt we owe them, to the extent that the trade deficit doesn't abate. That would be a nuclear option, so to speak, and should only be considered if the relationship gets so bad such that the economic exploitation by China, at our expense, becomes too great.

Finally, there is strength in numbers. Working with our allies in a coordinated fashion would be more effective than allowing China to pit us against each other on trade and other issues. The growth of China, its regional influence and control, along with its global economic prowess, is unstoppable. However, we can take actions to better protect ourselves that don't require the American consumer to be stuck with the bill. A carrot is better than a stick.

Russia

Never in Russian history has there been an attempt to treat the common man with fairness, free from exploitation. Serfdom, not freedom, has been the foundation of most of its history. Russia was ruled by a series of czars from the sixteenth century until the Russian Revolution in 1917.

With the writings of Carl Marx and Friedrich Engels in the mid-19th century, the proletariat, or working class, started to think that a different world was possible. *The Communist Manifesto* published in 1848 argued that capitalism would inevitably self-destruct and be replaced by socialism and eventually communism. It became the foundation for the modern communist movement. The Marxist movement found disciples in Vladimir Lenin, Joseph Stalin, and Leon Trotsky, leading to a bloody overthrow of the Russian government and the assassination of Nicholas II and his family in 1918, ending forever the Romanov dynasty and czarist rule.

That revolution ushered in what turned out to be a failed seventy-year socialist experiment that squashed self-motivated human achievement under the weight of communist socialist rule and corruption. The Soviet Union officially died in 1991 and Boris Yeltsin became the first freely elected leader of the newly independent Russian state. But that era lasted for only a decade. For the last twenty years, Russia has been led by Vladimir Putin, who recently achieved a political achievement that makes him eligible to be Russia's leader until at least 2036. He will be eighty-four years old.

When the former Soviet Union collapsed in 1991, its riches were largely stolen by a variety of oligarchs who became billionaires, many of whom collaborate with Putin, who himself is thought to be worth billions of dollars. Probably the most important thing to consider in terms of Putin and Russia today is the fact that Putin believes the worst thing that happened to Russia in the 20th century was the collapse of the former Soviet Union—not the starvation of millions of largely Ukrainian Russians in the 1930s at the hands of Joseph Stalin, or the 25-30 million Russians who perished during the Second World War. Putin's priority is to re-establish the old Soviet boundaries. His taking of the Crimea Peninsula in 2014, and attacks in Ukraine, are all part of his grand scheme.

In addition to his territorial conquests, Putin wishes to destabilize the West and increase his own posture. Interfering with the elections of other countries, including our own is just part of it. Any success in weakening the West is a win for Putin.

Russia has also stepped up its influence in the Middle East. Up until the Israeli-Egyptian peace agreement in 1979, Egypt was an ally of Russia as a part of the competition between the West and the former Soviet Union. The tanks Egypt used against Israel in multiple wars were Russian tanks. Now, like Iran, Russia has significant influence in Syria with troops on the ground. As I wrote earlier, when the U.S. decided to withdraw from supporting the Kurds in Syria, a traditional ally of the U.S., Russia was quick to fill the void. Russia isn't afraid of a nuclear Iran, as their missiles will be pointed toward Israel and the West, and not Russia. This is another example of how, for not a lot of money or risk, Russia continues to expand its influence at our expense. And it continues to advance its military capability. Russia is already reported to have ballistic missiles that can evade the most sophisticated of defenses in the U.S. arsenal. Our Department of Defense is working feverishly in order to overcome this vulnerability.

So, what do we do? Russia will respond to severe economic pressure. First, we should be fully funding and supporting NATO. Denying Russia access to global markets, financial and otherwise, would likely be the most effective way to influence its behavior. It would have to be well thought out, and coordinated, over a sustained period of time, in order to have any likelihood of success. Russia is a nuclear power and therefore has the ability to cast a larger shadow than its shaky economy can justify. It also has allies in China and Iran, and there is strength in those numbers.

While we don't have much control over how Russia operates in the rest of the world, we certainly do inside our borders. We must aggressively put an end to Russian interference in our elections, and it needs to be a bipartisan effort. Vladimir Putin has effectively secured control of the Russian government for the rest of his life. We should not allow him to control ours.

Iran

In order to understand the threat that Iran poses to the U.S. and our Western allies, one must be able to separate Islamism, an ideology of conquest, and Islam the religion. Islamism comes out of Islam, but it doesn't define Islam. And the vast majority of Muslims are not Islamists, militant or otherwise.

Without getting bogged down in an abbreviated, detailed history of the key historical events before we begin a discussion of Iran, I invite you to read "A Brief History of the Middle East" located in the Appendix of this book.

Iran is attempting to establish a large permanent Shiite Caliphate stretching from the western shores of the Mediterranean, east through Lebanon, Syria, Iraq, and beyond, with its center being Tehran. To that end Iran uses Syria, Hezbollah in Lebanon, and Hamas in Gaza, as militant and propaganda proxies, having supplied them with money and munitions, including the more than 160,000 rockets that Hezbollah and Hamas are reported to now have in their arsenal. Iran also supports terrorist activities in Iraq, Afghanistan, and Yemen, aligned with Al Qaeda and the Taliban.

Most dangerous of all, Iran is moving ever closer to having the ability to weaponize a nuclear warhead. It has successfully developed the capability to enrich uranium to weapons-grade material, along with the ability to deliver it via ballistic missiles already capable of hitting Eastern Europe. They are a huge threat to the United States and all of our allies in the region, including Israel.

The Iran Nuclear Deal, or the Joint Comprehensive Plan of Action (JCPOA), which was agreed to in the summer of 2015, was intended to encourage Iran to give up its nuclear ambitions in return for lifting economic sanctions and joining the community of peaceful nations. The parties to the negotiations included the U.S., Iran, China, France, Russia, the United Kingdom, the EU, and Germany. It didn't include Israel or the surrounding Sunni nations such as Egypt and Saudi Arabia, the countries that feel the most threatened by a Shiite nuclear Iran.

There were at least two fatal flaws with the agreement. First, the so-called rigorous inspection requirements did not allow the International Atomic Energy Agency (IAEA) to inspect Iran's military bases. To compound that failure, only "declared" sites were approved for inspection, not "undeclared" sites. It is at these "undeclared" sites where it is suspected nuclear weapons work was being conducted prior to the JCPOA. The IAEA could inspect these "undeclared" sites but only after giving

Iran almost a month's warning and delaying the inspection for more than seventy days—plenty of time to move or hide your nuclear weapons research. German publications report that Iran's attempts to buy nuclear technology continued and even increased after the deal went into effect.

Another major flaw is that *all* of the restrictions on the development of nuclear weapons sunset by 2030. The JCPOA, in exchange for slowing Iran's advancement toward a nuclear weapon, actually gives Iran license to achieve nuclear capability. We are already a third of the way there. Iran is investing in missile research and expects to have an intercontinental ballistic missile capable of reaching New York and Washington, by 2030.

As part of the deal, a freeze was lifted on $150 billion in Iran's assets being held mostly in foreign banks. Iran has used the money to expand its military presence and terrorist activity support in the region, including in Syria, Lebanon, Iraq, Yemen, and the Gaza Strip.

In 2018, President Trump unilaterally withdrew the U.S. from the JCPOA and has stepped up other U.S. sanctions to put pressure on Iran. With the American withdrawal, Iran stepped up its violations of the accord in earnest. The IAEA reports that Iran is increasing its stockpile of low-enriched uranium and is continuing to enrich uranium to a level of purity higher than allowed under the JCPOA.

If Iran obtains a nuclear weapon, it will have the unfettered ability to expand its Shiite dominance across the Middle East and beyond. It will be able to directly threaten not only Israel, but Europe with continental ballistic missiles it has already tested. Instead of making the Middle East safer from nuclear threats by eliminating an Iranian nuclear program, the failure to do so has ignited a need felt by its neighbors to develop their own nuclear weapons programs in self-defense. Nuclear proliferation will therefore likely accelerate in the region if Iran's nuclear ambitions are not contained. It was recently reported that China is helping Saudi Arabia develop a nuclear program. The Middle East Arms race is on.

Israeli Prime Minister Benjamin Netanyahu has declared that Israel will never allow Iran to obtain nuclear weapons. In fact, Israel has its own non-proliferation policy called the Begin Doctrine. It allows Israel to conduct preventative strikes against enemies with weapons of mass destruction programs. Under the doctrine, Israel has, for decades, quietly destroyed nuclear and chemical facilities across the Middle East. Israel is poised to take action if its allies won't, and might even be assisted by countries like Saudi Arabia to prevent the threat of a nuclear Iran.

The ruling Iranian clerics believe that by developing a nuclear weapon, they will secure the longevity of their regime by insulating themselves from outside forces and attacks, because their adversaries would be too frightened by the prospect of a nuclear retaliatory attack. They believe it is vital to their existence.

Therefore, perhaps the only way to get them to change their minds and behavior with regard to the development of nuclear weapons remains to convince them that instead of securing their regime, a nuclear weapons program will lead to its demise. And that can only happen, in my mind, and in the minds of many military commanders and experts, through a combination of crippling economic sanctions and a direct and last resort credible military threat. Peace through strength, as Ronald Reagan would say.

Economic sanctions against Iran, by themselves, aren't going to convince the clerical regime to stop their weapons development program. That's because the regime is willing to have its population suffer severely in economic terms, as a price to achieve their nuclear ambitions and regional territorial conquest. That is their history. They aren't hiding it.

A nuclear Iran is just one of many global threats emanating from militant Islamists. Whatever the solution to reversing the intolerant and radicalized militant part of Islam it seems that, at best, it will take a very long time. If we start right away, it could take a century or more. So, I am taking on the role as a bit of a hopeful futurist.

Here are five ideas for consideration, in order to be successful in reducing the long-term threat emanating from militant Islamism movements:

1. The West must wean itself from Middle Eastern oil so the world stops paying its enemies billions of dollars to have the resources to kill our men and women in uniform. The U.S. has made progress in this area. Since 2013 we have produced more oil domestically than we have imported. We stopped importing oil from Iran in 1991. Half of U.S. crude imports now come from Canada. Meanwhile, we should continue to develop renewable energy sources and solve the energy storage problem, leaving Iran increasingly isolated with stockpiles of oil it cannot sell.

2. Only when the world comes together to fight the militant Islamists the way we came together to fight the Nazis will we have a chance to prevail. Apparently 9/11 wasn't enough. And hopefully it won't take one or more detonations of weapons of mass destruction in the West, nuclear or otherwise, before that alliance materializes. The world needs to come together and isolate rogue regimes, like North Korea and Iran, to the maximum extent possible. Imagine how different the world would be had Nazi Germany invented an atomic weapon before D-Day. Likewise, our world could change forever should Iran be successful in developing and deploying a nuclear arsenal.

3. We can't fight the militant Islamists on our own. But we can help moderate Muslims fight them. However, the moderates within the Islamic community have been intimidated for millennia by a succession of leaders suppressing any independent desires or

will. They will need help—lots of it, that they can rely on for a sustained period of time. So far, we haven't begun to offer that. We displayed weakness when the Green movement tried to take hold in Iran in 2009. All we offered was weak and worthless verbal support. Regime change sponsored by the U.S. and its allies would likely cost us too much in terms of blood and treasure. However, regime collapse from within is a much more realistic goal. At a minimum, we could accept a continuation of the Iranian clerical regime, as long as it doesn't ever pose a nuclear, or other weapon of mass destruction threat, such as biological weapon production, and as long as it abandons its regional military conquests. The Islamic community is perhaps the last major world community yet to overcome their own tyrannical leadership and embrace humanism.

4. Moderate Muslim men need to protect Muslim women. Period. Sadly, there is no visible movement in that direction in any meaningful way. But that doesn't mean there isn't the opportunity for something like this to take hold, with the world's help and support.

5. And finally, perhaps the most effective way to modernize the Islamic world is through support of a global women's rights movement—a movement that isn't focused just on Muslim women but can take hold on the beachheads of what could ultimately be an emerging path to modernity in the full Muslim world. It could be among the most powerful influences in reshaping what it means to be Muslim. It would also hopefully diminish the scourge of global sex trafficking, which by itself is a moral imperative for the world. Perhaps the West could be a haven for Muslim women seeking equality and liberty.

I understand this is a lot easier said than done. But my conclusion is that anything short of these kinds of actions will have the world suffer from militant Islamism indefinitely.

All peoples deserve the protection of their basic human rights, civil liberties, and dignity. Nobody among us should be judged because of their race, religion, creed, or sexual orientation. When Muslim Americans speak of being cast negatively in the same light as militant Islamists, they have a right to complain.

However, I believe they also have a responsibility to recognize that their religion has been hijacked by militant Islamists who use terror as a common practice. They have a responsibility to condemn the actions of terrorism with the conviction of any peace-seeking community. The brave Muslim Americans who have put on an American uniform, or who speak out forcefully against Islamic terrorism, are among the righteous. They represent the best of their community and are leaders on the path to peace. We should all take a lesson from the Black Lives Matter movement in recognizing that silence is a sin.

I don't pretend to offer a full view of the global challenge represented by the threat from Iran in particular and militant Islamists in general. But hopefully, in this limited number of pages, I have helped to frame the discussion in a different way than has been customary within the national dialogue. And again, please read the Appendix, "Brief History of the Middle East," should you wish to do a deeper dive into the origins of Islamism.

CHAPTER 15

A VISION FOR AMERICA

When I speak with young people, particularly students, and those who have faced special challenges, I offer the following perspective:

With all of the incredible science technology that the United States has built that allows us to send probes into space on missions that last for decades, and view our galaxy and others through the Hubble Telescope, we have never found evidence of life anywhere in the universe. Imagine how lucky and privileged we are to be alive on a living planet, and how lucky we are to be alive today, at a time with so many advancements we enjoy in the modern era. On top of that, we get to live in the most amazing country in the history of the planet. As an Alaskan, I can add that I get to live in the most amazing state in the most amazing country, on the most amazing planet in the universe. We may face many challenges, like poverty, lack of equal opportunity, and a thousand other forms of pain, but we are still lucky to be here with the opportunity and responsibility to work toward a more perfect Union. It is all up to us.

Even though this book has largely been a critique of our flaws, and what we might have to do in order to set things in a better direction,

Americans are still just about the luckiest people in the history of the world. Thank you, U.S. Soldier.

America never stops moving forward. There is enough good, enough opportunity, enough liberty, enough practice of the rule of law, enough good democracy, that America is still the land of opportunity that attracts people from all over the world. And because we have the freedom and liberty to work hard to gain the fruits of our own labors and take risks, the opportunity for success has no limits. We are the country, after all, that reached for the moon, and now reaches for the stars.

But as far as we have traveled on that long road of advancement, we still have a long way to go in order to reach our full potential. There is too much poverty, too much hunger, too much injustice, too much inequality, too much pollution, too much disease, too much wealth disparity, too much crime, too much corruption, too much in the form of foreign threats, too much racism and prejudice, too little education, and too little strong and intelligent leadership necessary to solve these systemic problems.

With the right ideas, leadership, and courage, we can solve all of the problems we face. We defeated the Nazis and the Japanese at the same time. We went to the moon, and beyond. We invented the airplane, the semiconductor chip, the iPhone, and a cure for polio and other infectious diseases. We can solve these problems if we have the collective will to do so, because there isn't anything we can't accomplish that we set our minds to. That is what makes us Americans.

Imagine a country where we have a true meritocracy and everyone has an opportunity to reach their own potential.

Imagine a country where we help solve the global climate change challenges, including solving the energy storage problem.

Imagine a country where people are measured only by the content of their character and not the color of their skin.

Imagine a country where we have clean water wherever we need it.

Imagine a country where everybody who is able-bodied has a guaranteed job that pays enough to provide for themselves and their families.

Imagine a country where trickle-up is the order of the day, and not trickle-down economics.

Imagine a country where poverty is eradicated.

Imagine a country where adequate health care is available for all of our citizens.

Imagine a country where our Social Security system is sound.

Imagine a country where we convert criminals into law-abiding, self-reliant citizens.

Imagine a country where mental health is as important as physical health.

Imagine a country where gun violence is contained.

Imagine a world where the threat of Islamism is contained.

Imagine a world where nuclear threats and other weapons of mass destruction are contained.

Imagine a world with fair international trade.

Imagine a world where there is peace between Israel and the Palestinians.

Imagine a world where we cure cancer.

Imagine a world with less broken glass.

And imagine a country where our democracy thrives because we have a fair election process that elects the most capable people to serve the public at large instead of special interests.

Politics is the art of the possible. It is up to an educated voting public to demand from our elected officials that all of these things that we can imagine, come to be. We the people can make a more perfect Union. It's up to us. All of us.

Finally, I would like to thank those who made it possible for me to have lived my life as I have and be able to present my opinions to you. All of the liberties we enjoy have been earned through the blood and sacrifices of the U.S. Soldier. I again salute and thank all of our men and women in uniform, and all of those brave men and women who came before them. First, I want to thank my parents Barney and Natalie, along with my loving stepmother Rachel, who entered the concentration camps, at age four, after losing her parents in the death camps after the Gestapo came to their Krakow family home, and took them away from her. She ultimately immigrated to America and thrived in the greatest country the world has ever seen. I'd like to thank all of the people in my life that I have been blessed to know and love, and whom I am blessed to call my friends. And especially John and Donna Tracy, whose dedication to help this book get published was invaluable. And most importantly, I want to thank my children Sarah and Jeffrey, for helping to make me a better person.

Thank you for your time. Thank you for your interest, and for buying this book. God bless America, and God bless the U.S. Soldier.

APPENDIX

A Brief History of the Middle East

A More Perfect Union is a safer one. Of the threats facing the United States and the West, the conflicts in the Middle East have to rank very high, including our own domestic vulnerabilities to acts of terrorism like 9-11, hijackings, oil supply disruptions, cyber-attacks, and as much a threat as any, the threat of a nuclear Iran with inter-continental ballistic missile capability now likely within a visible time horizon. The threats are growing. They have reached our shores, and they're not going away.

So how did we get here, and what can we do about it? The answer to how we got here is complicated, as it took over a thousand years. And the answer to what do we do about it has to start with how we got here. So, in order to advance the discussion about solutions to problems emanating from the Middle East, we need first to understand at a base level what the problems are, and from whence they came. And that requires perhaps at least a short history lesson or reminder. We have to study history before we can learn from it, in order to avoid repeating its mistakes. So, I will take some time here to summarize what I understand to be the key historical circumstances that have most contributed to creating the current threats facing the United States and many of our Western Allies.

I am not a foreign policy expert. But I am an American who has been fully engaged in trying to understand the battle to defend ourselves against militant Islamists, and who has been participating in the politics of that battle for decades now. Working closely with some of our elected officials, I am grateful that they sometimes listen to what I have to say. I have been focused on this issue since I was in my thirties. I am sixty-five now. And most of what I have learned has come from learning from others, by reading books by respected authors and listening to scholars and experts who are much more accomplished and knowledgeable than I will ever be on this subject. I have also had many firsthand experiences and have been a living witness to history. So, I won't profess to be a scholar, but I believe I understand the basic tenets and history of the West as it relates to Islam. I will share with you what I have come to understand, recognizing that some of the history I describe will certainly be open to some debate. However, I will forge ahead knowing that most of what I express can be found in the public domain through legitimate sources.

As such, I must give special recognition to several of my teacher/authors. I would highly recommend that the reader seek out some of their writings-authors including Bernard Lewis, Dennis Ross, Robert Spencer, Robert Satloff, Ayaan Hirsi Ali, David Makovsky, Michael Makovsky, Bret Stephens, Robert Baer, and Ishmael Khaldi. Along with my decades long friend and Middle East guide, Sarit Mayer. I must first thank them for helping to expand my understanding of a very deep history and set of problems. My early religious schooling, the writings of these authors, the teachings of others, and my focused observations have framed my understanding of history and the path we are on. I have been to the Middle East eighteen times. I do take a considerable time on this subject, because of its importance and its level of complexity. The intersection of historical context and current reality matter.

Many who might read this book will conclude that I operate with a prejudice against Islam and Muslims, in favor of Israel and the Jews. To the contrary. Foundationally, I am a humanist who believes that all humans, as much as possible, should be able to advance themselves and their families, on an equal footing. I believe in the Golden Rule, that one should treat others as they wish to be treated. If we all did that, the world would be a much better place. So, my strong position, being a Jew myself, is that Israelis should not be denied their own country, just like the Arabs of Palestine, or Palestinians, should not be denied one themselves. I would like the Palestinians to be able to live in their own state, safely, next to their neighbors in peace and harmony—just not at the expense of their neighbors, particularly Israel.

The recorded history of human civilization in the Middle East goes back thousands of years, and there are many versions of that history. Much of the history was not written down and was passed orally from one generation to the next, until a written history could be established. There is of course the Torah, the Jewish Bible or First Testament, parts of which were written more than 2,500 years ago. This was followed by the Christian Bible, written almost 2,000 years ago. And then there is the Koran, written 1400 years ago, along with its interpretive companion book, the Hadith. The following brief description represents, to the best of my knowledge, what is generally accepted as being close to the truth among historians and academics, with some commentary along the way. I expect some readers to challenge some of my writings, and probably rightfully so.

Even though Man's existence in the region predates where my story begins, I will start about 3,500 years ago, or 1,500 BCE, Before the Common Era, when the seeds were planted for three of the great religions of the world.

The Jews were the first recorded peoples to give up paganism and embrace the belief in only one, and an Almighty God. Roughly 3,500 years ago the Jewish people were held as slaves by the Egyptian Pharaohs who used Jewish slave labor to help build the Pyramids. After being led to freedom to the Promised Land by Moses over 3,000 years ago, the Jewish people roamed the desert for forty years, finally settling in the Land of Canaan, with Moses delivering the Ten Commandments from Mt. Sinai along the way. Canaan, which was largely a deserted region that had been referred to as Mesopotamia in ancient times, later became known as Judea, with Jerusalem, or Zion, as its capital. The settlement was founded by King David 3,000 years ago. Shortly afterwards, the Jews built their first Holy Temple. After 500 years of surviving as the center of Jewish religion and culture, in 586 BCE the first Temple was destroyed by the Babylonians. Many Jews were forced to flee their country out of fear of persecution and death in what became the first Jewish exodus from their ancestral homeland. Some of those fleeing persecution wound up in Africa, including Ethiopia. Starting in the 1980's, the Jewish descendants of those who took part in the Exodus following the destruction of the first temple, started to return to the land of Zion, or Israel. Operations Solomon and Moses brought thousands of Black Ethiopian Jews home, after thousands of years of living in the diaspora, having fled to safety from persecution endured for generations.

About fifty years after the destruction of the first temple, it was rebuilt. And, again, the new Jewish Holy Temple became the center of Jewish religion and culture for another five hundred years, until the arrival of the Romans. In the first century the Roman Empire defeated the over 1,000-year-old nation of Judea, destroyed its Holy Temple in Jerusalem and exiled hundreds of thousands of Jews. Rome needed to impress the Persians, another great warrior nation (now Iranians) that they could control the inhabitants of Judea, so as not to appear weak. To erase all memory of Judea, Rome renamed it Palestine, after the Israelites' biblical enemy, the Philistines. That was the start of the second historic exodus by Jews away from their homeland, the land of Zion.

For hundreds of years, until the 1970s, the people who are now referred to as Palestinians were called Arabs of Palestine. In fact, it wasn't
uncommon to refer all residents of Palestine as Palestinians, including
Arabs of Palestine, but also Jews and Christians of Palestine. That was
until Yasser Arafat, the terrorist leader of the terrorist organization the
Palestine Liberation Organization, (PLO), was taught Nazi propaganda
techniques by Soviet KGB agents in Romania in the 1970s. This was revealed in an op-ed piece by one of those former KGB agents, in the *Wall
Street Journal*, almost twenty years ago. In essence, if you tell people a lie
often enough, they begin to believe it. In order to create the mythology
that the Arabs of Palestine had the deepest historical roots to the region,
he hijacked the name as being exclusively the traditional name for those
who were most commonly referred to as Arabs of Palestine. Arafat rightfully expected that people around the world would think that Palestine,
instead of being named by the Romans as previously mentioned, was
originally named for his people. Pretty clever of him, in a very sinister
way.

Yasser Arafat created this mythology because he knew he couldn't win
in the West with the truth, on moral grounds, or by the sword. The current Palestinian leadership, in order to continue to advance their agenda
of intolerance and demonization of Israel, is resorting to what is too much
a part of the non-democratic culture in the world, including the Middle
East, and that is lies and propaganda. It's as effective as much for internal
purposes as external ones. The current PLO Chairman and Palestinian
President, Mahmoud Abbas, refuses to come to the negotiating table
to negotiate a two-state solution with Israel. It's because the Palestinian
leadership still doesn't accept Israel's right to exist as its own state living in
peace and security as the homeland of the Jewish people. Accepting a seat
at the negotiating table in order to create a two-state solution would be
an acceptance of defeat, in the minds of the Palestinian leadership. There
is only one Jewish state. There are twenty-three Muslim states. They plan
on a twenty-fourth, believing that the land was stolen from them, first by

the Crusaders, and then the West after the First World War. That is what they were taught, and time is on their side. It took centuries the last time for Islam to essentially eradicate the Christian West from Jerusalem and its surroundings, to then be held for almost seven hundred years, until the collapse of the Ottoman Empire in 1917.

Getting back to history, what you may not know is that the Colosseum in Rome, paid for largely by the treasures stolen from the second Jewish Holy Temple, was also largely built by slaves from Judea. There were 20,000 Jewish slaves brought from Judea to Rome after Judea was conquered.

For the two millennia after the Roman conquest, no other state or unique national group developed in Palestine, and no ruler chose Jerusalem as its capital. Instead, different empires and peoples came, colonized, ruled, and disappeared. Jews continued to inhabit the region throughout all these times and changes.

Going back in time once again, we have the birth of Christ—a Jew, a reformer who railed against accepted traditions in search of a new form of humanity, which ushered in ultimately the development of the power and influence of Christianity, and the Catholic Church in particular. As we know, Christianity has been a powerful influence for millennia throughout Europe, North and South America, and parts of Africa, with a current religious following of about 2.3 billion people. Islam has 1.9 billion, and Hinduism 1.2 billion. There are only about fifteen million Jews worldwide. It's about the same number there was before the Holocaust. It has taken seventy-five years to recover from having lost 40% of our people in the extermination camps.

Later, in 571 AD came the birth of the Prophet Muhammad and then his teachings through the Koran, starting in the 7th century. The Prophet Muhammad was not born in Israel. He never visited or lived in

Jerusalem, and of course never stepped foot on the hill where the Dome of the Rock sits, one of the most holy sites in Islam—it is a mosque that was built on top of the destroyed Second Jewish Temple as an historic symbolic act of desecration and of staking a claim. The Koran teaches that Muhammad ascended to heaven from Jerusalem. He was a very charismatic and successful warrior leader, and he conquered large parts of the region, as did his descendants and disciples following his death.

Muhammad's empire grew rapidly and widely. Within a hundred years of his death, Islamic influence spanned from Spain to Indonesia, including many parts of Europe.

The reason that Muhammad and those who came behind him were so successful in expanding their rule was because of these Five Pillars of Islam, and how they were administered.

1. First, to be considered a Muslim, one simply has to declare faith and loyalty to God and his Messenger Muhammad.
2. Secondly, one must give charity to others.
3. Thirdly, there is the commitment to prayer. Strict adherents are supposed to pray five times a day, but it isn't a requirement in order to be a Muslim.
4. Fourth, there is the fast during Ramadan.
5. And fifth is a pilgrimage to Mecca, something only a small fraction of the almost two billion Muslims accomplish in their lifetimes.

This simplicity—coupled with the threat that those who were conquered, and who wouldn't convert, would either be subjugated, enslaved, or killed—was a powerful inducement to join the faithful. Other than that, different cultures were pretty much left alone, so there was no serious resistance.

For this short history lesson, we'll continue with the split in Islam after the death of the Prophet Muhammad. A key distinction between Shiite Muslims and Sunni Muslims is that Shiite Muslims believe the legitimate authority over Islam was to be established from within Prophet Muhammad's direct family blood line, whereas their archrivals and adversaries, the Sunni Muslims, started as disciples of Muhammad, but came to recognize others as legitimate religious leaders. For over a thousand years, there has been a lethal Islamic family feud. In fact, as part of this rivalry, a Shia direct descendant was killed in the historic Battle of Karbala in 680 AD. Ever since then, there has been a holy blood feud between the Shia and Sunni, in which the Shia feel that their leadership in the Muslim world was cheated from them. Shiite Iran is committed to regaining leadership by successfully establishing a Shiite Caliphate, with Iran at its center.

For almost a thousand years, Islam had great influence in the Middle East, extending to Europe and even to East Asia. Only about 20% of Muslims live in the Middle East; however, the majority of militant Islamists live there. They believe that the West's presence in the Middle East over the last thirteen hundred years has come and gone, and come again, and will leave again. By force.

The Christian Crusades took place in order to recover the Holy Land from the Muslims in the 11th, 12th, and 13th centuries. Tragically for Christians, the Crusaders lost, and they ultimately had to retreat. Centuries later, the Ottoman or Turkish Empire ruled the region as a Sunni-based Islamic Caliphate for four hundred years until the end of the First World War. Between 1517 and 1917, Palestine was an unimportant backwater of the sprawling Ottoman Empire, which at its height in 1683, covered vast parts of the Middle East, North Africa, and Eastern Europe. Palestine was separated into small sub-districts within the large province of Syria, and later Beirut. The Palestine region initially prospered under the Ottomans, but during the Empire's decline, was mostly reduced to a sparsely populated, impoverished area.

After a thousand years of influence, Islamic control started to wane, in Europe in particular. In the 17th century, parts of Islam started to embrace certain cooperation with the West, and there was relative peace.

Coincidentally, perhaps, after spending hundreds of years without a country Jews could call their own, a new modern movement of Zionism was established in Europe in 1897 by Theodore Herzl, an Austrian. A movement by world Jewry to re-establish a homeland for the Jewish people in Palestine ignited. It started a process of migration back to the homeland of the Jewish people that eventually culminated in the establishment of the Jewish State of Israel in 1948. Between 1878 and 1914, over a hundred thousand acres of land was legitimately purchased by Jews from willing Ottoman Turks and Arabs of Palestine sellers of land.

However, when the Ottoman Empire, as an ally to Germany, was defeated in World War I, its foreign lands were ceded to the victorious Allies. Just as the Allies carved new nations out of Europe's defeated empires, so too they carved nations out of the former Ottoman Empire and created most of the Middle Eastern states we know today, including Iraq, Lebanon, and Syria. They also redrew Palestine's boundaries and officially recognized it as the Jewish National Homeland. The newly formed League of Nations set up "Mandates" that had Britain control the areas largely known today as Israel, Jordan, and Iraq, with Syria and Lebanon being governed by France. These Mandates were to be maintained until such time as the indigenous populations could be self-governing.

In the famous 1917 Balfour Declaration, Britain endorsed "Zionist aspirations" to re-establish a homeland in Palestine and promised to facilitate the effort. In 1920, international peace negotiators incorporated the Balfour Declaration in the Treaty of Sèvres, and called for a Mandate in Palestine. In 1922 the League of Nations instructed the British Mandate authorities to facilitate Jewish immigration and settlement of Palestine. Many European and Arab leaders hoped Jews would revive this small, impoverished and thinly populated region. Jews were being encouraged by the world to resettle in Palestine.

However, later in 1922, in response to Arab pressure, Britain abrogated the Mandate and cut off 77% of Palestine in the first of multiple reductions in the size of the Jewish homeland to come, granting it to the Hashemite Kingdom in what would become Jordan. Ruled for forty years by King Hussein of Jordan, starting in the 1950s, Jordan is now ruled by his son King Abdullah, viewed as a somewhat modern and moderate monarch. Today, over 70% of Jordanians are Palestinian Arabs and not Hashemites, which causes plenty of problems for the young king. There are also hundreds of thousands of new immigrants seeking refuge from a war-plagued Syria.

Another very important movement that developed was the Muslim Brotherhood, established in Egypt in 1928 by a schoolteacher by the name of Hassan al-Banna. The Muslim Brotherhood started out as a self-help organization, but the true goal was to defeat the West and establish a new global Islamic world order based upon Muslim supremacy. Al-Banna was assassinated in 1949.

Then we have the rise of Hitler and the Third Reich in the 1930s, and World War II, along with the implementation of the Final Solution. This was the plan for the complete extermination of the Jews of Europe, otherwise known as the Holocaust. Hitler might have gotten away with it if it were not for the United States military, the boys who courageously hit the beaches of Normandy, along with General George S. Patton and the brave men of the Third Army, along with the other millions of heroic combatants in that war. The heroes of the Greatest Generation also include the men and women at home producing the instruments of war. They saved the world from tyranny. We owe them so much.

As a result of hundreds of years of persecution and atrocities suffered by Jewish people, culminating in the Holocaust, the world came to a reasoned, fair, and just decision regarding the Jewish people and the Middle East: that the Jews unquestionably deserved a Jewish homeland to where they could immigrate in safety, and that home should be their ancestral home, with Jerusalem as its capital.

Being respectful of the rights of the other indigenous population, the Arabs of Palestine, in 1947 the UN passed Resolution 181, partitioning the remaining Palestine Mandate between Arabs and Jews. The wish for a two-state solution was finally legitimized. The Jewish portion had a Jewish majority. Jewish leaders accepted it even though their portion comprised only 13% of the original Mandate, and more than half of the land was the arid Negev Desert. President Harry Truman was the first world leader to recognize the young Jewish state, shortly after the UN resolution was passed.

However, Arab leaders from Egypt, Lebanon, Syria, and Jordan rejected the offer and instead incited the Arabs of Palestine population living among the Jews to leave and join their armies poised to attack the new Jewish State with the goal of eliminating it. It would have been the second of a one-two punch to kill and exterminate the Jews, after the Holocaust's first massively deadly punch. This ideology is what in part defines the Holy War, or Jihad, which the militant Islamists wage against the West still today.

Getting back to the Muslim Brotherhood, after the assassination of Hassan al-Banna, his successor, Sayyid Qutb, who was even more radical, expanded the movement. Later seen as a threat, he was also killed, by the President of Egypt, Gamal Abdel Nasser, in 1966. But that assassination helped to ignite a global Muslim Supremacy movement that has significant repercussions to this day. In fact, Saudi-based Wahhabism led to the establishment of Al-Qaeda, a competitor to the Muslim Brotherhood in the quest to defeat the West in its own back yard. Remember, Osama Bin Laden led Al-Qaeda, and the 9-11 attack. Al-Qaeda's goal is to make the cost of cooperation, especially by Saudi Arabia, with the West, so high that they will break their ties with us.

In fact, once the U.S. retreated from Iraq, Abu Musab al-Zarqawi built and grew Al-Qaeda in Iraq, causing untold death and destruction. Another outgrowth of the Muslim Brotherhood was the group Islamic State of Iraq and Syria, or ISIS, led by Abu Bakr al-Baghdadi. Both Baghdadi and Zarqawi were killed by U.S. forces, though before his death, Baghdadi promoted the idea of independent attacks against the West by believers, without the need for any contact with the ISIS mothership. That is one reason we have seen many attacks in the U.S. in recent years. This is all to say that the Muslim Brotherhood lives on in its quest to destroy the West. Another child of the Muslim Brotherhood is Hamas in Gaza.

In order to add texture, and to better understand the forces and influences in the region, it is important to understand better some of the key players. Islam is not a monolithic religion. It has its sects and cultures. For example, Iran is a Muslim country, but not an Arab country. It is Persian. The Persians, under King Leonidas, fought the Greeks 2,500 years ago, but ultimately failed to defeat and rule Greece. Iran is also a Shiite Muslim country. Its neighbors, Saudi Arabia, Egypt, and Jordan, are largely Sunni. Iraq has large Sunni and Shiite populations. 80% of the world's Muslims are Sunni. In Saudi Arabia, another offshoot of the Sunnis is the Wahhabis, another radical sect that has an alliance with the House of Saud, the royal family. As a point of reference, a member of the Islamic faith is a Muslim. The ideology that seeks the destruction of the West is Islamism. And the militants who participate in that battle are called Islamists or militant Islamists. It is very important not to generalize about Muslims as being Islamists, as the vast majority are not.

Through an alliance, the House of Saud has allowed the Wahhabis control over the Saudi Arabian school programs, or Madras, in exchange for Wahhabi cooperation with, and the legitimizing support for the royal family and the House of Saud. As a result, fifteen of the nineteen hijackers in the 9/11 attacks came from Saudi Arabia.

Again, a key distinction between Shiite Muslims and Sunni Muslims is that Shiite Muslims believe the legitimate authority over Islam must be established from within Prophet Muhammad's direct family line, whereas their competition and adversaries, the Sunni Muslims, started as disciples of Muhammad, and at times have accepted secular leadership, such as the Caliphates that ruled Islam during the Ottoman Empire.

This separation goes back to early descendants of the Prophet Muhammad more than a thousand years ago. And the only peoples they each historically oppose more than each other, are the infidels, those who do not accept the Prophet Muhammad as their spiritual leader—in other words, the West, a world that the militant Islamists want to destroy. In that quest they will use terror attacks, airline hijackings, mortar rockets into Israel, and suicide bombers. The world witnessed these terrorist operations against Israeli athletes at the 1972 Munich Olympic games, the first attack on the World Trade Center in 1992, and the 9-11 attacks, which killed nearly 3,000 Americans. There have been attacks against our Marines in Beirut, attacks against our military in Iraq, and attacks against the *USS Cole*. The terror campaign has spread to Brussels, Paris, and Mumbai. On and on it goes. And now we have Shiite Iran on a path to a nuclear weapon, and ISIS is re-organizing. This battle has now come to our shores in repeated attacks such as at Fort Hood, Boston, San Bernardino, and Orlando. Americans fear there is more to come… because there is.

It is important to remember that Israel is the only truly democratic country in the region, led by citizenry that freely elects its leaders. Both

Turkey and Egypt have elections, but in Turkey's case, President Erdogan has compromised the military's ability to ensure that elections are free, secular elections. He threw secular generals in jail who weren't willing to cooperate. And now, after a sloppy coup attempt a few years ago, he has placed thousands of his countrymen into their prisons in order to keep them out of his political way.

Let us pause and remember that freedom isn't the same as democracy. Freedom of religion, assembly, and speech can be achieved without democracy. But democracy doesn't work unless there are established institutions that protect the rights of minorities and provide for free and fair elections. There is not a part of Muslim history that has embraced these Western values. It is a key reason why it is so difficult to achieve free elections in Muslim countries, unless there are seismic and historic shifts in the attitudes toward the rights of women and other human rights.

The bottom line is that in the Middle East, with the exception of Israel, there is not a separation between church and state. Therefore, religious minorities are vulnerable. Israel is the homeland of the Jewish people, but it has institutions and courts that have a strong history of protecting the rights of all minorities, just as America does. Israel's Christian population is growing. The opposite is true in all of its neighboring countries. Of approximately nine million residents of Israel, 6.8 million identify as Jews, almost two million are Arabs, and about 180,000 are Christians.

I don't use the word terrorists, in describing those who perpetrate acts of terror on behalf of global jihad, because it isn't descriptive enough. The term Radical Islam at least identifies a root source, but it suffers from being open to criticism because it generalizes about peoples of the Islamic faith, instead of focusing on the culprits themselves: militant and radical Islamists. Those radicalized individuals within the Islamic faith, or who align themselves with Islam as a vehicle to accomplish their goals, and who work with other like-minded people, choose to engage in the most heinous acts of terror in their quest to create a growing Islamic Caliphate. Their goal is to spread Sharia law, where women are subjugated to men, slaves are subjugated to believers in the Prophet Muhammad, and infidels are subjugated to all—to be converted, controlled, or killed. According to some interpretations of the Koran, this jihad pauses only for the purposes of re-arming and preparing for the next battle.

Militant Radical Islamists don't represent a majority of Muslims, by a wide margin. But the 10 to 15% they do represent number at the hundred-plus-million level. So, they represent a very significant global and powerfully dangerous militant force. Their Jihadist cause, also, unfortunately, preys upon the weak, and often mentally challenged, but certainly those with violent tendencies, in order to recruit them to their ranks. Even if just 1% of those in the militant Islamist camp choose to join ISIS, Al-Qaeda, and other terror organizations, that's still a very sizable force of a million warriors.

The fact that the Sunnis are killing the Shiites, who are killing ISIS, who are killing Al-Qaeda, as Islamic conquest competitors, doesn't detract from the main theme. The elimination of the West, and of Judeo-Christian values from the Middle East, are common goals shared by them all. And for the followers of the teachings of the Muslim Brotherhood, from the world itself. We are already in a form of World War III. It just isn't the kind of war that we are familiar with. The Viet Nam War was a war we didn't know how to fight or to win. But the current war is like the Viet Cong guerilla fighters on steroids, in terms of global reach.

The 3,000-year journey to this point has been long, hard, and often cruel. We are indeed in a war with aligned global forces engaged in militant conquest around the world, leaving no continent untouched. It's not a war like World Wars I and II, when we could easily identify who the bad guys were, and why. It isn't a war principally about borders, but ideology, and good versus evil. It is a kind of war that we don't yet know how to fully and effectively fight. It is a war against modern barbarism. I call it modern barbarism because the perpetrators use modern weapons in their recruitment drive for their soldiers, and in the lethal weapons and methods they use. Their goals and ideology allow them to recruit soldiers who are willing to decapitate the heads of living humans, and to burn a Jordanian pilot alive, for example. Some call it a clash of civilizations. Some call it the War Against Radical Islam. Whatever you call it, it is a war where powerfully dangerous and deadly forces from a variety of militant states and organizations, all of whom claim to have roots in Islam, are waging a jihadist war of terror against the West, at home, and abroad.

Iran, Al-Qaeda, ISIS, the Taliban, Boko Haram, Hezbollah, Hamas, the Wahabis of Saudi Arabia, the Muslim Brotherhood, and others that most people haven't heard of are all, in one form or another, expressing their intolerance of Western norms and values, by engaging in a terror war of attrition against the West.

Islam has not evolved from its roots in a world still living in the Middle Ages, the way Christianity, as a religion, evolved and accepted peaceful secularism. As does Israel, and Egypt, the most populated Arab country, for the time being. Morocco is also evolving positively. But the rest of the region, from Libya to Afghanistan, and Yemen to Saudi Arabia, are all ruled by non-democratic Islamic-ruled dictatorships or monarchies, where Islam is the country's official religion. It seems like a double-edged sword. Strongman leaders maintain civil control, often through brutal measures. The intolerant history of Islam generally hasn't allowed for democracy to gain any traction because a thriving democracy requires the protection of minorities and women, and that they are treated equally. These are values absent in the Middle East, with the exception of Israel.

What they have in common is a shared ancestry in terms of the teachings of Muhammad, which includes the Koran, and its all-important companion document, the Hadith, the combination of which represents collective teachings of the Prophet Muhammad.

It is how those of the Islamic faith have interpreted these writings differently that has generated different sects. Scholars write that the Koran and the Hadith are so diverse in their teachings that individuals can select and adopt certain teachings and interpretations to suit their own beliefs, or agendas, as the militant Islamists have done, claiming to be the correct messengers of Muhammad's teachings. Muhammad, and the Koran, are somewhat respectful of the Torah (The Book) and the Christian Bible, as the seeds that led to the ultimate ascension of Islam as the supposed religion of the highest order.

Another central facet of Islam is how women are treated. On the one hand, as other religions preach, pre-marital sex is taboo, in large part because of the need to avoid unwanted pregnancies. It is also true in Islam. But the subjugation of women is deep and exploitative. Not only are girls not allowed to attend school by and large, they must wear a hijab to cover themselves in order to avoid bodily exposures that could excite men. Many are partially sexually mutilated. It also, for example, takes three women to equal a man's testimony in legal disputes.

But one of the pronouncements by the Prophet Muhammad has resulted in horrible treatment of women today, and it has to do with one of his wives. Muhammad had many wives. But one of his favorites, as it was recorded, was Aisha. As the story goes, Muhammad was informed by advisors that Aisha, on a trip away from him, had been unfaithful to him. So, he banished her. But then later, a more trusted advisor told him that the stories about Aisha were untrue. Therefore—after consulting with the Almighty, of course—Muhammad decreed that if someone is to be convicted of adultery, there must be two male witnesses able to testify as such. The consequence is that today there are thousands of Iranian women in jail who are victims of rape. Having had pre-marital sex, albeit forcibly, and not being able to produce two men in actual witness to the rape, they are imprisoned for violating Sharia Law.

Muslim women are taught that separate is equal, so to speak—that some privileges they have regarding dowries, for example, compensate for the otherwise unequal treatment they get. It appears to be a religious/cultural form of brainwashing. You will find Muslim women defending their treatment, presumably as a result of centuries of forced indoctrination or out of fear.

Even though Europe, and now the United States feel directly threatened by a variety of terrorist organizations, they pale in comparison to what we will be facing from Iran in the decades ahead if Iran is not held in check in terms of its nuclear development program and regional encroachment. ISIS, the Taliban, Hamas, and the Muslim Brotherhood, all don't pose a substantial threat to our national security. However, Iran does.

In 1953, the United States supported a coup d'état in Iran that displaced its leader with the Shah of Iran. The shah was a strong ally to the West in the Cold War against the Soviet Union. So, there has been an historic animosity toward America by many Iranians because of it. One of them was the Ayatollah Khomeini, who in 1979 successfully orchestrated a revolution that put his Shiite theocracy in place, and held American Embassy personnel hostage for 444 days, until after Ronald Reagan took the oath of office.

Relations deteriorated even further in the 1980s during the eight-year Iran/Iraq war in which the U.S. backed the Iraqis because of our strained relationship with Iran. What we didn't realize is that in the end we weren't so much working to support an ally, or hoping to help stabilize an important oil- producing region of the world, as much as we were stepping unintentionally in between the old rivalry between the Sunnis and the

Shiites. The Sunnis and Ba'athist party, led by Saddam Hussein, controlled Iraq, which also happened to be inhabited by millions of Shiites as well. I hope you now appreciate how serious the problem of Iran and its nuclear ambitions are. Now to the second major Middle Eastern issue.

Peace Between Israel and the Palestinians

The true tragedy of the Palestinian people is that they are forced to have leadership that forces them into a perpetual, unwinnable war of extermination against Israel and the Jewish people, which takes a tremendous amount of their resources, leaving them economically deprived. This suffering is then used in a global propaganda campaign in order to gain sympathy and to delegitimize and weaken Israel through the global BDS (Boycott, Divestment, and Sanctions) campaign, in addition to an almost continuous barrage of security infringements across its borders. There are over 160,000 rockets estimated to be facing Israel from Gaza, led by Hamas and Lebanon, largely controlled by Hezbollah. Hezbollah is a Lebanese-centered terrorist group also dedicated to the destruction of Israel and supported by none other than Iran. In the view of militant Islamists, in their quest to eradicate all infidels from the Middle East, Israel is in the way

The primary reason there has never been peace between Israel and the Palestinians is the lack of a unified Palestinian government that is willing to recognize Israel's right to exist as the homeland of the Jewish people, within safe and secure borders. This violent rejection of a two-state solution is manifested through the Palestinian leadership in Gaza under the control of Hamas, an offshoot of the Muslim Brotherhood, and the Palestinian Authority, or PA, representing West Bank Palestinians. Hamas gets strong terrorist support help from other anti-Israel sources, but principally from Iran. For seventy years, the Palestinian leadership has rejected a two-state solution, and instead has supported and engaged in a deadly, brutal, and immoral war of attrition against Israel since its inception, and has not paused since, in its quest to destroy her, except to re-arm, as the Koran teaches.

In one relatively recent episode in 2014, Hamas had incited Israel to re-enter Gaza with a strong military force by kidnapping an Israeli Defense Forces (IDF) soldier, and launching thousands of rockets into populated areas in Israel, after which there was a cease-fire implemented, resulting in Hamas being allowed to begin receiving materials, including cement and other construction materials, to rebuild buildings destroyed in the short defensive incursion by the IDF. Hamas instead used construction materials meant for schools and houses to build intricate tunnels that were discovered, poised and equipped with electricity and other material, in preparation to send hundreds of fighters into Southern Israeli public neighborhoods for mass killings.

Israel has allowed these materials to go into Gaza, with reservations, because of the history of the materials meant for schools, roads, and other facilities, diverted instead for the death tunnels. In April of 2016, the Israeli Defense Forces destroyed tunnels discovered that were more than a hundred feet deep, built with the thousands of tons of cement supposed to be used for peaceful purposes. In the north, late in 2018, with the help of tunnel detection technology jointly developed by the US and Israel, Israel was able to detect and secure a terror tunnel twenty-two stories below the ground! The tunnel was fully plumbed, with electricity and all the means necessary in order to launch a massive intrusion into Northern Israel, in order to kill and kidnap as many Israelis as possible.

The result is that this rejection of a two-state solution by the Palestinian leadership has left the Palestinian people all too often trapped in poverty, hopelessness and despair. This is because the militant Islamists are not willing to tolerate the establishment of any non-Muslim and democratic country in the Middle East, and instead uses all of their resources—including young suicide bombers at times—to destroy Israel.

It's what explains the global BDS, or Boycott, Divestment, and Sanctions campaign that is intended to weaken Israel. This all is partly a continuation of the millennia-old battle between the Arab and Muslim forces and Judeo-Christian values, and for Islamic hegemony control of the region.

The constant war against Israel, and the resulting self-destruction it creates in Gaza, makes it impossible for any successful economy to develop. The unemployment and despair that results from the hopelessness of a never-ending war against Israel provides Hamas with vulnerable juvenile targets to exploit, by channeling the programed anger that goes along with despair, into militancy and suicide bombing attacks. They exult suicide bombers as one of the only desperate means at their disposal to fight their battle of liberation, when the simple answer, instead, is a willingness to live in peace among their Jewish neighbors.

Everything therefore needs to be examined in the context of a continued war by aggressors, who for more than seventy years have fought a hopeless and immoral battle, one that brings much more suffering to its own people than to Israel.

Egypt made peace with Israel. Jordan made peace. And it was hoped that the Palestinians of the West Bank wanted to make peace. But Palestinian President Abbas, years ago, announced the rejection of the Oslo Peace Accords signed in 1994, by Israeli Prime Minister Yitzhak Rabin and PLO Chairman Yasser Arafat. He has been inciting violence as well, and paying the families of martyred suicide bombers, and those in Israeli prisons, for acts of terror.

Even though the vast majority of Israelis support a two-state solution, where Jews and Palestinians have their own countries, most Israelis don't view peace as being a reasonable likelihood anytime in the foreseeable future, because they know they have no partner in peace, now or on the horizon. It's not that Israelis don't support an independent Palestinian state, it's just that they realize current Palestinian leadership, instead of seeking peace, continues to seek Israel's destruction. Israelis know what ovens look like. The Palestinian leadership continues to incite hatred for Jews, and continues to attack Israelis any way they can, including economic boycotts, to knife attacks, stone-throwing, suicide bombers, rockets, and advanced terror tunnel networks emanating from the Gaza Strip—even incendiary balloons. My own nephew, Ari, two years ago, while serving in his Israeli Defense Forces reserve unit, was stabbed six times by a terrorist in Northern Israel. He fought him off and survived but will be scarred for life, both physically and mentally. He is a brave and courageous young man.

To remind you again, I am Jewish, in the spirit of full disclosure, so I don't wish to mislead anyone. I am working with an active prejudice. I want Israelis to be able to live in peace and harmony among their neighbors. I want that for all of their neighbors. But in particular, I don't want my own people to be cruelly left out of that human opportunity. That is my prejudice.

Golda Meir, Israel's first and only woman prime minister, remarked almost fifty years ago that there will be peace with the Arabs of Palestine when they love their children more than they hate the Jews. Those same children are still being trained, beginning at early childhood, to aspire to hate Jews, and to become martyred suicide bombers. The prime minister also remarked that if the Arabs of Palestine were to drop their weapons, there would be peace. But if Israel dropped its weapons, there would be no Israel. How prescient a set of statements those were, way back then. She also was reported to have responded to a question as to how Israel was able to successfully confront the many large forces that it is surrounded by, and which threaten it, to have said, "It is because we have a secret weapon; we have no place else to go."

The three most important statements that I can make about the complex subject are: (1) The Palestinian leadership, and their regional supporters, have not accepted Israel's right to exist within safe and secure borders. (2) Every official and non-official act they do, whether it appears to be a concession or not, is to advantage their position in the long run, to destroy Israel. (3) And since they can't win their arguments with the truth, or by force, they are trying to destroy Israel through the use of lies misinformation campaigns, the rewriting of history, and other propaganda techniques. This includes economic boycotts, divestment campaigns sanctions, and applications to the International Criminal Court all as a campaign to discredit Israel. At the United Nations, more condemnations are passed against Israel than almost all other condemnations combined, including against Iran, Syria, Russia, China, and North Korea. With special emphasis on American campuses, Islamists are trying to isolate and weaken Israel. In fact, in much of the Muslim world, deceitfulness and lying are accepted forms of communication by governments. That is a critical way in which their governments maintain autocratic control.

Let's be clear. The Palestinians, like all peoples of the world, deserve to enjoy a country of their own, and to live in peace and harmony among their neighbors—but not at the expense of denying that to others. And that is what the Palestinian leadership is demanding. The problem is that multiple peoples have inhabited the same area for thousands of years. Therefore, the only real solution to two peoples having historic ties to the same land is a two-state solution: a homeland for the Jewish people, and a homeland for the Arabs of Palestine. It took decades for the Israelis to come to that conclusion, in part because the home for the Palestinians was supposed to be part of Jordan. But the Palestinian leadership has never accepted even the most generous of peace offers.

By signing the Oslo Accords in 1993, Yasser Arafat and Yitzhak Rabin committed the Palestinians and Israel to a two-state solution. But Arafat's signature turned out to be a ruse. In 1999, at the end of the Clinton Administration, the Palestinians were offered their own sizable country, with water rights, and even parts of East Jerusalem for their capital as part of the deal. But Arafat rejected it and instead initiated the Second Intifada, the systemic killing of innocent Israelis on buses and in night clubs, where suicide bombers would propel deadly metal objects through the brains and limbs of innocent Jewish infants, children, old men and women, and anybody else they could kill, maim, and mutilate.

There are twenty-three Muslim countries, where Islam is the official or dominant religion of the country, including Turkey, Egypt, Iran, Iraq, Lebanon, Jordan, Syria, Libya, Kuwait, Yemen, Qatar, United Arab Emirates, Afghanistan, Pakistan, Abu Dhabi, Saudi Arabia, Uzbekistan, Morocco, Tunisia, and Indonesia.

But there is only one homeland for the Jewish people. The militant Islamists (we must include Hamas in Gaza, and Mahmoud Abbas, the President of the Palestinian Authority, to a lesser extent, in that group) want to destroy Israel either militarily, or preferably, by imposing a one-state solution, where Israel will be transformed into the twenty-fourth Muslim Sharia Law country. It represents another form of the Nazis' Final Solution to get rid of the Jews for the second time in less than a hundred years, even while there remain thousands of aged Holocaust survivors.

Likewise, Islam will be taking Europe by birth and migration over the next hundred years, if trends continue. They won't need the sword. That is one reason the vast majority of Israelis want a two-state solution, because they know demographics will work against them over time. Today there is little prospect for peace in the foreseeable future, because the peace the Palestinian leadership still wants, and requires first, represents a path to the destruction of Israel. Issues to be negotiated, like settlements and Jerusalem, strategically become pre-condition demands, as excuses not to even agree to meet. Fortunately, there are some shifting sands in the desert that could be a catalyst to a change in the trajectory for peace between Israel and the Palestinians. More on that a little later.

Traditionally, Israel has had no territorial ambitions beyond its legitimate borders. After being recognized in 1948 as the homeland for the Jewish people, a fraction in size of what they were offered in the first quarter of the 20th century, all of the increases in size were a result of winning defensive wars against aggressors. They won the Sinai Peninsula from Egypt after the Six Day War of 1967, when Moshe Dayan won a decisive tank battle victory while being far outnumbered by a Russian-tank-equipped Egyptian army. However, Israel gave the Sinai back to Egypt when the great Egyptian President Anwar Sadat made the courageous decision to make peace with Israel. That peace has held for more than forty years. Israel also ceded territory lost in bloody battles against Jordan, when King Hussein made peace with Israel, a peace that has also endured.

But since then, when the Israeli Defense Forces retreated from Lebanon after being attacked and establishing a security corridor, they didn't get peace as promised, but instead suffered thousands of rockets launched and pointed toward Israel's civilian population centers. And when it withdrew from Gaza, a hornet's nest of militant Islamists, it didn't get peace, as promised. Instead, Israel got suicide bombers, more rocket attacks, kidnappings of its soldiers, and tunnels built for the purposes of launching deadly attacks against civilian populations—and more recently, swarms of hot air kites delivering fire bombs on agricultural areas have caused much damage. If there is a two-state solution agreed to, these past aggressions are a key reason Israel will no longer accept sharing Jerusalem, because they know they could be putting their enemies at their doorsteps.

There are four issues that all parties recognize have to be resolved in order for there to be peace between the Israelis and the Palestinians. They are:

1. Borders have to be defined.
2. Reliable security has to be established.

3. Any role for the Palestinians in Jerusalem needs to be defined.
4. And a resolution must be established for the hundreds of thousands of Palestinian refugees who have been held largely in poverty in UN refugee centers in Lebanon and living impoverished in neighboring countries. Tragically they have been living that way for more than seventy years because their leaders preach to them that if they can't have all of the land, they can't have any of it, and because none of the other Muslim countries, including Jordan, have been willing to accept them as permanent and equal citizens.

I will address each issue very briefly, even though they each have many complexities associated with them beyond the scope of this effort.

Each side deserves a country and a set of borders they can protect. The so-called "Green Line" represents the borders that were established at the end of the Six Day War in 1967 when Israel was surrounded and attacked by its neighbors. Israel was making strong advances in gaining territory in a defensive war. But at the urging of the Arab League, the United States convinced Israel to stop advancing its tanks. Where the tanks stopped, the borders were drawn, disregarding the natural and historic separations between Arab and Israeli villages. That has been a problem ever since, as has been the lines drawn by France and Great Britain after World War I, in the creation of Lebanon, Syria, Jordan, and Iraq. Israel has offered to give up, and get land, so that the borders can be contoured to solve this problem. Just where the borders need to be is generally recognized by all parties. But the Palestinian leadership rejects any solution that doesn't expose Israel to destruction. Never again will the Jews subject themselves to their own destruction.

Israel is not attacking its peaceful neighbors, but its intolerant militant Islamist neighbors are attacking her. Limiting an Israeli military presence to its own border with a Palestinian West Bank won't be sufficiently secure, because Israel can't trust current and future Palestinian leaders to secure their own borders and prevent militants from using the West Bank as a staging ground for attacks against Israel. That is why Israel needs enhanced security guarantees. And as we know, peace with some of its neighbors doesn't grant Israel peace with all of its neighbors.

A very big issue, but a false one, has to do with what is referred to as the settlements. Israel has several settlement blocks or cities in the West Bank, in one of the two territorial areas set aside for a Palestinian State. The other is the Gaza Strip. The settlements in the West Bank of the Jordan River have become an insidious propaganda tool used by the Palestinian leadership in their continuous attempts to paint themselves as underdog victims of a so-called occupation. Let's be clear: the primary goal of the Palestinian leadership is the destruction of Israel, the homeland for the Jewish people. Some may challenge this statement, but they are unable to offer concrete examples that the Palestinian leadership has offered Israel or done anything to advance a secure two-state solution for both sides.

As mentioned before, one of the key issues is borders. In any negotiation, both parties come to the table with demands. In the end, neither side gets all they want. Success is usually achieved when one side gives up something that is of lesser importance to them than the other side, and receives in return things that are more important to them. Hopefully on balance, both come away being winners of the most important things to them, where a balanced compromise is achieved. It is that balance that gets the deal done, not the isolated decision on just one factor. This is the way the world works.

Part of a practical solution is for Israel to exchange comparable land used for the settlements for the Palestinians, as opposed to abandoning large population centers. Land swaps will be necessary in order to contour boundaries around traditional Arab versus Jewish villages. These settlement blocs have become a deep part of the Israeli fabric. The Palestinian position is that Israel is always expanding the settlements and is therefore expanding end-game territory unilaterally.

It is true that Israel has historically constructed homes on adjacent land to the settlements as part of organic growth in a community. It is a tiny country no bigger than New Jersey, with a growing population, and it needs room for its inhabitants. Israel expects to give up similarly valuable land as the areas where the settlements are located, in future fair land swaps as part of an overall peace agreement. But the Palestinians have also historically required a freeze in settlement construction as a pre-condition to entering negotiations, in effect, requiring an important bargaining concession just for showing up.

No negotiations operate in this way, and their approach is a clear message that the Palestinian leadership wants the other side to know they aren't serious about a two-state solution. The freeze restrictions that have been demanded were even to prevent a homeowner from adding a room on top of their house for a newborn baby, or family marriage, in some cases, defining even the roof of a home as a border in advance of any negotiation. It makes their deceit and insincerity about a true two-state solution transparent, for those paying attention. But the lack of progress continues to be feed-stock into their victimization global propaganda campaign, and their efforts to delegitimize Israel within the world community, as a path to their one-state solution. For much of the world, this campaign is successful, because those with anti-Semitic prejudices convert Israel's need to take action to protect itself in a hostile neighborhood as inhumane acts against the Palestinian people.

As an illustration, in 2010, Prime Minister Netanyahu went to his cabinet, because of an appeal from President Obama, to institute a settlement construction permit freeze on the West Bank, as a measure of goodwill. It was done in the hopes of facilitating the bringing the Palestinian Authority to the bargaining table. It was reported there was a big debate within the cabinet. In the end, the prime minister was granted a ten-month freeze, without the authority to extend it. It was a gesture, backed up with skepticism that Israel would get anything for its offering.

After nine months of the ten-month settlement freeze, President Abbas announced that in order for him to come to the bargaining table, the freeze would have to be extended even further. His ploy was revealed, and the Israeli Cabinet's cynicism was validated. Ever since then, Abbas has made more overtures to Hamas, the terrorist organization that controls Gaza, than he has in working toward a two-state solution. He has never been willing to sit down at the bargaining table because that would represent an admission that they could accept some negotiated result that would leave Israel secure. Peace with Israel is a non-starter for them. Allowing Israel to survive is a show-stopper.

Instead, the Palestinian Authority is engaged in a worldwide campaign to delegitimize Israel and its right to exist, by promoting the BDS campaign of boycotting Israeli products, urging governments around the world to divest in any investments in Israel, and the application of economic sanctions, along with votes at the UN to have a two-state solution unilaterally imposed on Israel. Such an imposition, Israel believes, would help lead to its own destruction.

Twenty years ago, Israel was prepared to grant the Palestinians some sovereignty in Jerusalem. But after decades of lies, attacks, and suicide bombers since then, that comfort level has evaporated. I think the only way to offer the Palestinians a piece of Jerusalem is to start a referendum process in Israel. The first referendum would start twenty-five years after there is a bona-fide peace agreement, and the Palestinians stop teaching hatred of the Jews to their children. The Palestinians will have twenty-five years to prove to the Israelis that the peace is a sincere peace. Then if the Israelis feel secure by letting the Palestinians share their capital, then so be it. But if the referendum fails because the Palestinians have failed to give the Israeli population that comfort, then the Palestinians will have another ten years to prove they are sincere about peace with Israel, and another vote could be taken. If the Palestinians want a piece of Jerusalem, they have to legitimately offer and live a true peace with Israel.

And finally, there is the question of what to do with Palestinian refugees—the remnants and descendants of those who were lured away from Israel during the War of Independence in 1948 in order to join the armies of the enemies of Israel so they could combine forces and push the Jews into the sea. As soon as the United States gives Texas back to Mexico after defeating the Mexican Army, after Europe cedes itself to Germany after Germany lost the Second World War, and we cede the rest of our country to Japan as reward for us defeating them, then I guess Israel should cede its territory to the Palestinians refugees who want to destroy it. Well, life doesn't work that way. The home for the Palestinian refugees should be in a secure and independent Palestinian state, and in other Muslim countries in the region that should welcome them as part of a fair and historic solution for a suffering people. Instead, thousands are held captive in UN camps, where resentment and militancy are promoted and fester.

Also, the idea of referring to Israel as an Apartheid State, as some claim, is offensive and revolting. When I am confronted by someone who refers to Israel as an Apartheid State, I then offer that they must then believe that the subjugation and exploitation of an entire ethnic population, as white-ruled South Africa treated its black indigenous population, is the same thing as protecting your family from annihilation, which is what Israel is faced with. That usually ends the conversation.

But in terms of any likelihood of a peace agreement between the two parties anytime in the near future, it is true that a large portion of Palestinians appreciate the opportunities for jobs and living conditions in Israel, but that tells only part of the story. A ten-year study by the

Washington Institute for Near East Policy found that Palestinian support for peaceful coexistence with Israel has eroded over time.

Results indicate that a majority of Palestinians living in Gaza, the West Bank, and East Jerusalem increasingly say that a two-state solution should not mean the end of conflict with Israel. Rather, around 60% would opt to continue the struggle to liberate all of historic Palestine, "from the river to the sea."

The surveys also revealed growing discontent between the Palestinian people and their own government, the Palestinian Authority and Hamas.

The study found that the number of Palestinians who support conflict with Israel over annexation has declined in the past year, partly because they do not trust their leaders to conduct the confrontation successfully. And a majority of Palestinians surveyed said they support specific forms of economic cooperation with Israel. Two-thirds of West Bank respondents also reject the practice of paying Palestinian prisoners in Israeli jails, a signature Palestinian Authority policy.

Taken together, the survey indicates the majority of Palestinians would prefer that their government focus on domestic reforms and economic development rather than on Israel, though if given the opportunity, they would still prefer to "liberate" Palestine and eliminate Israel.

But as I suggested, the sands are changing. A combination of the Palestinian leadership's lack of willingness to come to the peace table, and the heightened threat from a Shiite nuclear Iran that the Sunni Gulf nations feel, is creating a big change in thinking in the region, at least for some of the Gulf Sunni nations, who have long been aligned with the premise that any path to stability and an advancing of a Muslim agenda has to start with successfully advancing the Palestinian cause of eliminating Israel. However, today, for a growing number of Sunni nations in the region, their fear of a nuclear Shiite Iran transcends their normal distaste for the Jews and support for the Palestinian cause. Their patience with the Palestinian intransigence in coming to the peace table is wearing thin for the first time, because of the Iranian threat. That is what recently led the United Arab Emirates(UAE), Bahrain, and Sudan to make peace with Israel and establish all normal forms of diplomatic relations.

It has been twenty-eight years since the last Muslim country, Jordan, made peace with Israel. In an odd twist of political and military dynamics in the Middle East, Israel is starting to become viewed as an asset as opposed to a liability, because Israel is viewed as a source for important technologies, and they share a common threat in Iran.

Still, there won't likely be a peace agreement between Israel and the Palestinians until the Palestinian leadership takes positive and constructive steps in the peace process and stops teaching hatred to their children, starts loving them more than they hate the Jews, and drop their guns. Israel would need to respond likewise by offering significant rewards, and by allaying concerns of the Palestinians regarding any mistreatment. Until that time, Israelis continue to work hard to create an amazing life in an amazing place, undeterred by the always serious threats just on the other side of their borders, and all too often, within sight. Hopefully, if there are multiple successes in Sunni nations deciding to establish diplomatic ties to Israel, it could lead to a widening tolerance for Israel to stay in the region, successfully, and at peace with its neighbors.

And the last point I will make here is in response to Iran's long claim and interest in pushing the Jews into the sea in order to create a single Palestinian State. Do you think that if Iran is successful in developing a nuclear weapon, and drops it on Israel, which is a stated purpose, that the radiation will stop at the Gaza border? The truth be known, Israel is more concerned about the well-being of the Palestinian people than Iran is.

ABOUT THE AUTHOR

David Gottstein is President of Dynamic Capital Management. Growing up in his family's pioneering grocery business in Alaska, David earned a degree in Economics and Finance from the Wharton School. He has fifty years of successful business experience, including supply chain management and logistics, and the wealth management business. He is founder and CEO of Efficient Tax LLC, the nation's leader in delivering tax-sensitive wealth management software that is focused on true after-tax returns as opposed to tax minimization strategies.

He also has over fifty years of experience in the public policy political arena as an activist, starting with his stuffing of envelopes for the "All the Way With LBJ" 1964 presidential campaign, when he was ten years old. Seventeen years later, he became an aide to the Alaska State Senate President, where he learned the value and sophistication necessary to be able to work effectively in a bi-partisan manner.

He was a founding member of "Backbone," a non-partisan political alliance formed in 1999 to protect Alaska's oil interests from exploitation by multi-national oil companies. In 2007 he helped bring the Alaska Legislature together to pass a progressive oil tax, during the Administration of Sarah Palin.

A student of Middle Eastern history, David has traveled to the region eighteen times. He continues to live in Anchorage, Alaska where he raised his two children, Sarah and Jeffrey, in a place he considers the most amazing state, in the most amazing country, on the most amazing planet in the universe.

9 780578 240107